Got The Powers.com

Ten Ways To Phenomenal Success

· ·

Big Big Value Bonus Inside and on Website
www.gotTHEpowers.com

GotThePowers.com – 10 Ways To Phenomenal Success

www.gotTHEpowers.com

Copyright © 2016 Susan Phenomenal Powers

ISBN: 978-1540317124

Publisher
10-10-10 Publishing
Markham, ON
Canada

Printed in Canada, the United States of America and United Kingdom

| Contents |

| **Dedication** |

To my late mother, for always living in the moment, making life an adventure and being such an inspirational, intelligent, and compassionate lady.

My late grandparents, for their love, kindness, laughter, and being inspirational to me.

My fabulous friends, you know who you are.

| Foreword |

Do you feel like you are spending your days working to pay your bills, with a life that is anything but VIP? Susan Phenomenal Powers has broken down aspects of your life into manageable sections and created a plan that is easy for you to follow. She takes you on a fun and imaginative journey, from health and beauty to your finances. Susan turns larger tasks into workable goals that you can easily accomplish to see real change in your life.

gotTHEpowers.com delivers more than just a to-do list. Susan gives you the inspiration you need to live your VIP lifestyle and the tools to make it happen. This is more than just a short term fix – it is truly a change in your mindset and actions that will lead you to the life you have always dreamed of.

I enjoyed reading Susan's down to earth take on daily life and how life seems to be in fast-forward. By applying the principles Susan outlines here, you can take your life out of the fast lane and into a speed that allows you to truly enjoy yourself. She is a great coach and mentor who bottles her unique wisdom in between the pages of this book. Enjoy the journey!

Raymond Aaron
New York Times Best Selling Author

| Introduction |

I want to welcome you to the first step in living a VIP life. I have worked with individuals as a life style consultant and entrepreneur, helping them to develop their personal and business skill sets to achieve the best versions of themselves. I am passionate about helping people, but I know that if you aren't grabbing people's attention, they aren't going to retain or implement it.

My strategy for my clients is simple and empowering, because I want to help you create a custom plan for your life and have a bit of fun in the process. Throughout the pages of this book, I am going to cover a wide variety of topics, from health to wealth and nearly everything in between. As I do, I hope you will be inspired to take these strategies and implement them into your own life.

Use this book to create a plan that will let you live the VIP life that you always imagined. It is possible, if you are willing to act and claim it for yourself. With the tools I am going to give you, it will be possible for you to take the next steps to realize a deeper and more meaningful life, both personally and professionally.

The important thing to remember is that it starts with you. Never doubt that you are capable of achieving great things in your life. The biggest obstacle you will ever face is your own unwillingness to change. Once you conquer that, anything is possible. So let's get started!!

CHAPTER 1
VIP HEALTH

| **Chapter 1** - VIP Health |

The first area to we have to cover is your health and wellbeing. Let's face it, if we don't make time to take care of ourselves, we will never be able to take care of anyone else or achieve our dreams. This means going beyond just making sure that we eat right. It means caring for our body in a variety of areas. The benefits go beyond the physical and encompass our mental wellbeing as well.

Imagine for a moment, a young mother with 5 children. Three of her darling miracles are 5 and under. There are sports and after school activities for her older children, play dates and day care for the younger ones. Add in a full time job and the necessary tasks involved in making sure everyone is clean and fed, plus general upkeep on her home and you have one busy and stressed out mom.

Her schedule is very full. But nowhere in that list was any time for just mom. Instead, it was completely full of activities that are focused on others. Many of us can relate, even if we don't have large families. There is the pull of parents that need our help as they age, our children who need our guidance and our spouses or significant others who need our attention and love. It is easy to see how taking care of ourselves can filter to last place and then off the list altogether.

Before you can even consider pursuing your dreams, you need to start by taking care of your body. After all, you will need it for the rest of your life. Plus, happiness research has proven time and time again that happiness and our health are connected. The healthier we are, the better position we are in to pursue what makes us happy. Our self-image and self-esteem are tied to what we see in the mirror, whether we are willing to admit it or not. When we let ourselves go, so to speak, by ignoring our diet and not scheduling time for exercise and hobbies or experiences that reduce our stress levels, then we are setting ourselves up to fail.

| **Energy, Radiance and Vitality** |

One of the first areas to consider is our energy level. Are you tired all the time? Does it feel as if you never get enough sleep, no matter how early you head to bed? The problem might be the fuel you are giving your body. Your metabolism is a function of the processes that your body has to complete to sustain life. When you are not providing the best quality diet, your body has to work harder to achieve the same results.

Overtime, there isn't any way for your body to maintain its processes, so it ends up showing the lack of nutrients in a reduction of your energy level.

Now you need to ask yourself, what am I putting into my body? Am I helping or hindering my own metabolism and energy level? We all have a basic idea of what is not good for us. A regular diet of fast food, for example, isn't going to be nutritionally sound over the long run. Chocolate can be great in moderation, but if we are living on it, then we might find ourselves struggling with a few extra pounds.

Of course, I can't tell anyone not to eat these foods ever again. Life happens and we are running late or just feel the need for a special treat. The question is what do we eat most of the time, so we afford an occasional splurge of our favorite treat? In a word, you need to avoid excessively processed foods. What do I mean by that?

Go to the frozen food aisle and pull one of the frozen microwavable meals out. Look at the number of ingredients and additives that are in just one of these meals. Next question, how many of them can you actually pronounce? Here's a good rule of thumb. If you can't pronounce it, then you likely should avoid eating it.

But it makes sense. The more processed a food is, the more preservatives and additives are being included. This means we are getting more than just the nutritional elements of the food that we are eating. We are taking in a larger number of chemicals. Study after study have shown that the chemical load on our bodies has increased dramatically in the last 60 years. Our environment has changed and this has impacted our exposure levels. It has also changed how much stress our bodies are under to reduce our levels of toxicity. Often, the chemical load can overwhelm our systems, making it easier for us to fall prey to disease, including viruses.

I am all for eating healthier and reducing my chemical load, you might reply, but I am no cook. How in the world am I going to eat? The processed foods are all that I know!

Walking into the market can feel like a real challenge if our main goal is to avoid the processed foods. Nearly every aisle is full of them. We talked about frozen foods, but you can go down any aisle and find a myriad of examples of processed products.

I would also like to point out that this processed lifestyle extends to what we drink to stay hydrated. There are plenty of coffee shops, carbonated drinks and many other less than healthy options to drink. Yet the caffeine that we are ingesting is having a greater impact on our ability to stay hydrated. Have you noticed that after a cup of coffee you are quickly thirsty again? Caffeine lovers take that as a signal for another coffee. It becomes a vicious cycle that leaves our bodies without the amount of water that they need to sustain life. Take the time to drink water regularly throughout the day. Your body, which requires water for virtually every process, will thank you by performing at its best. Trust me, you will feel the difference.

There is also a growing movement attempting to provide more fresh options or items with limited processing. Just check your local farmer's market. Fresh produce options are available, along with canned products, such as jam, honey and other options to fit anyone's taste. Organic options are available as well. Still, if organic pricing seems out of reach, be sure to clean your vegetables well. There are plenty of easy to use options that can reduce the chemicals on your fruits and vegetables, giving you better taste and flavor.

Even in a traditional supermarket, there are typically a variety of fresh food options. This includes fruits, vegetables and freshly butchered meats, including chicken and fish. Depending on our tastes and general cooking ability, there are plenty of recipes that can make it possible for us to eat healthy and enjoy what we are eating. I know we are all busy. Eating healthy can appear to be time consuming, but it doesn't need to be. You just have to be willing to do some initial homework to find the right recipes to fit your lifestyle.

The speed of our lives doesn't have to create an either/or situation regarding healthy eating habits. It just requires planning. Look at your life now. You have a multitude of activities, experiences and items that require planning to be sure that you get them completed. You figure it out, though, because those things are important to you. The same is true of making healthy choices. You need to be willing to decide they are important to you and then you will make the time to accommodate them in your life.

Supplements can also be a method of making sure that you are getting the proper nutrients. Keep in mind, however, that not all supplements are created equal. Some may claim to have larger amounts of different nutrients than they actually have. So do your homework before you purchase a supplement. Make sure that you know the company and the type of product they are producing.

Additionally, supplements are meant to do just that, supplement. That doesn't mean that you can make unhealthy food choices and then make up for it with a large number of supplements. Your body will not be able to maintain this type of lifestyle indefinitely and you will ultimately pay for it.

But a healthy lifestyle includes more than better food choices. You need to be willing to give yourself the right amount of sleep. Buy out the time for your minimum of 8 hours. Functioning at your best means giving your body a chance to make repairs and recharge. If you are overscheduling yourself and reducing your sleep time, then you are going to find yourself struggling to meet all those obligations and perform at your best. Then pursuing anything else can be overwhelming, especially our dreams and goals.

Eating right and getting enough sleep is key to pursuing our dreams and goals. If we don't buy out that time for ourselves, we can't refill our batteries. Ever been in a car when the battery has gone dead? It can't charge the car to start and you are essentially stuck. Don't let your battery get so worn down that you are stuck. Choose to buy out the time for your body and it will thank you by being ready when you need it.

Your body gives off a natural radiance and vitality. When you are not taking care of it, then you find that radiance and vitality begins to disappear. But what is radiance? According to the Merriam-Webster dictionary, radiance is defined as a quality of brightness and happiness that can be seen on a person's face. It is a warm, almost soft light that shines out from within us. I believe that if we are taking proper care of ourselves, then we are going to have our own radiance, which will reflect how comfortable we feel in our own skins.

Radiance goes hand in hand with our vitality. We give ourselves the power to pursue our dreams and goals, but without vitality, we can't pursue them with real energy. Our power comes when we take the time for ourselves. Are you choosing to care for yourself or are you going to keep putting yourself in last place? If you are in last place, your dreams will never be realized, because you won't have the energy to strive for them.

| Beauty and Endurance |

When we are struggling with a difficult situation, it can seem as if it will never end. This is when endurance comes into play. Endurance is the ability to do something difficult for a long time, including dealing with pain or suffering that may be a part of the situation.

Many times, we talk about how important beauty is, but often the focus is on our external beauty. I want to focus on our internal beauty. This describes the qualities we have that can help us to stay the course of making a significant life change or pursuing our dreams. If we don't have internal fortitude and a willingness to put forth the effort to grow and change our lives, then any change we try to make will be short-lived. After all, change is not easy and there will be obstacles. Without endurance, we won't be able to make a permanent change.

It would be great if making changes in our lives was as simple as saying, "I want to change my habit of chewing my nails," and instantly, we stopped biting our nails. However, it doesn't work this way. Often, we have to make changes to our routines and habits to pursue a goal or make healthy choices. But when we put in the effort and keep trying despite any setbacks, then we will see that change happen.

Think about keeping yourself healthy and happy. It requires effort on your part. Not only do you have to eat right, you have to exercise and get your body in motion. Regular checkups with your doctor can help you find potential problems and make adjustments in your diet or daily routine before it becomes a larger issue. The reality is that our internal and external beauty are based on our ability to endure and stick with the uncomfortable parts of change until we have created a new life for ourselves.

Do you feel confident and empowered in your life now? Or do you wish that you had a different life? When you lack the confidence to make changes in your life, then you will find yourself struggling to make large changes successfully. Instead, start with small changes in your routine. As you start to see success, then it can help you to build the stamina and confidence necessary to make the big changes.

Endorphins kick in when we have success and they can make us feel excited and happy with ourselves. The point of small successes is that we will soon be on a role to creating more significant movement in our lives.

There is a saying that we can fake it until we make it. Sometimes making our outside over can have a positive impact on our insides. Here are just a few tips to consider to create a VIP healthy lifestyle for yourself.

Tips for Women

- Take regular exercise classes to maintain a toned and healthy body.
- Cleanse, tone and moisturize to keep your face fresh and clean.
- Take regular supplements to maintain a healthy lifestyle and appearance.
- Exfoliate your skin 2 to 3 times a week to reveal brighter skin and get rid of dead skin cells.
- Use an eye cream to avoid puffiness and dark circles around the eyes.
- Keep nails clean and tidy and use clear or coloured nail polish.

Tips for Men

- Join a gym and devise an exercise program. Get into a routine of regular exercise.
- Always keep your nails clean and trimmed.
- Avoid letting your lips get chapped or dry by regular use of a lip balm.
- Exfoliate your face and body to maintain healthy skin.
- Take regular vitamins/supplements to ensure you give off the appearance of good health and fitness.
- Avoid the aging process by regular use of moisturizer with sun protection on your face.

If you take the time to take care of yourself on the outside, it will have a significant impact on your insides. The beauty within will be able to shine through and have an influence as you make significant changes to follow your dreams.

Finally, I want to talk about the process of transformation. It can be an exciting time as we achieve our dreams. But it also requires flexibility on our part. When one path or opportunity closes, we need to be open to other opportunities that present themselves. It takes strength to correct our course, but the effort is worth it. One way we can support our transformation is through a detoxification and education.

Now the detoxification that I am talking about is more than just cleaning toxins out of your system. It includes taking the time to detoxify our beliefs as well. What is our internal dialogue like? Our beliefs are formed by our thoughts and the perceptions we have of our experiences. So our internal dialogue plays a key role in our belief system. Therefore, we need to take the time to examine what we tell ourselves and why we believe it. If a belief no longer serves to move us forward, but limits us instead, then we need to be willing to detox and throw it out. Our flexibility will come into play here, because if we are too rigidly tied to our beliefs, it can have a negative impact on our ability to create the life we were always meant to have.

Another key part of transformation includes education. If you are pursuing a new way of life, you need to make sure that you are educating yourself on what that entails. Books like the one you hold in your hand are key to educating yourself on how to create change in your own life. Take the time to treat yourself well by reading, learning and growing. When you combine this with a healthy lifestyle, you will be able to produce the life you want and have the energy to pursue the things that you are passionate about.

Throughout this chapter, we have touched on a variety of areas where you can see ways to feel more vibrant, healthy and happy. This includes taking care of yourself mentally and physically. But taking care of yourself mentally involves not only changing your stress level and how you view stress, but continuing to learn and grow. Throughout the following chapters, we will be discussing a variety of ways that you can grow in terms of your education, your experiences and even your interactions with others. Taking care of yourself is a key first step, but along the way, you need to learn to have a positive impact on others in your life.

CHAPTER 2
VIP BEAUTY

| **Chapter 2** - VIP Beauty |

Feeling beautiful is not always easy when you are rushing through your life. As we discussed in Chapter 1, neglecting your own well-being can often mean that it becomes the lowest priority on your to-do list. Taking time to feel beautiful, however, can have a variety of benefits in terms of our mental and emotional well-being.

Still, it can be hard to find time to spend on our VIP beauty regime. In fact, we might find that we aren't giving ourselves the VIP treatment in this regard at all. How many of you have dropped off or picked up your kids from school in sweatpants and a messy bun? If you looked in the mirror, would you be willing to say you looked like you just rolled out of bed? Remember, you deserve to have some time to care for yourself before the day begins. If you don't, it can be hard to stay calm and centered when life starts throwing in all its curve balls.

At this point, I suspect that you are agreeing with me and are willing to sacrifice that extra 15 minutes in bed to do something to make yourself feel great all day. But how do I get that irresistible feeling in the morning? Many of us are not makeup artists and we don't have our own personal consultant who will pick out our daily outfit. In fact, just walking into a store that specializes in makeup, hair and their accessories can be overwhelming. So how can you get started?

| **The Skin You Are In** |

Start with your skin and makeup. In a variety of stores, there are consultants who can help you to assess your skin type and recommend the right skin care regime for you. Your skin is unique, so it may need special products to handle breakouts or dry skin. Once you find the products that work for your skin, make sure that you use them regularly. Washing your face on a daily basis can assist in getting rid of dead skin cells, dirt and removing makeup. Make sure that you remove your makeup every night to maintain optimal skin health.

When it comes to your skin, keep in mind that it is the largest organ in your whole body. It provides a natural barrier between you and the rest of the world. Protection from germs, bacteria and a host of other foreign invaders is also part of this organ's to-do list. Therefore, we will want to do what we can to protect and defend this key part of our body and one of the outward signs of our beauty.

It is not vanity to want to look good, but human nature. We all have that one look, which gives us a feeling of power. That power can be to feel cool and classy or hot and sexy. But for so many of us, this is a rare treat, something we only do for ourselves once in a great while. What a waste! You should be able to leave your house feeling your best every day, regardless of whether you are going to work, school or on a date. When we feel our best, it shows in our confidence level.

Now we come to the makeup you are using on a daily basis. There are quite a number of brands available and in a variety of price points. However, this is not an area to skimp on. Remember, we are talking about your skin. Let me ask you a question. If you found a product that was in your price point, but contributed to making your skin break out, is that product really worth putting on your skin?

There are so many of us who are doing just that by buying junk products, just because they are cheap. It doesn't mean that they are going to do the job, but it is almost a guarantee that you will need other products to correct what the original products did. Clogged pores can be a sign that your skin isn't able to breathe. Then you have to deal with the pimples and breakouts that come when your skin is being stifled. Therefore, it is important to find products that provide the coverage you want in terms of imperfections, while not contributing more problems. The best products hide what you want to hide and accentuate your best features, be your eyes, your cheekbones or your beautiful smile.

If you aren't sure what products are best for your skin, then it is important to consult a professional. There are plenty of places where you can consult with a makeup artist. When you do, be sure to explain exactly what is going on with your skin. Give them plenty of details. This will help them match you with the right skin care products to meet your needs. Your skin is unique. Although you may share a skin type with someone else, your skin will not necessarily react to products the same way that their skin does. Be willing to try something different in order to find what has the best outcome for you!

Now let's talk about those runway makeup trends. It is so easy to look at them and think, "I can do that!" or wonder, "How in the world do I do that?" Runway styles are exaggerated to make a statement that compliments the designer's vision. The reality is that most of us are unlikely to wear the makeup or styles straight from the runway. The idea is to take the runway look and translate it into something that is doable for our everyday lives.

If you want to take on a runway makeup trend, talk with a makeup consultant at your favorite beauty bar. They can help you to translate into a way that makes you feel gorgeous and sexy, while at the same time, avoiding the more outrageous and impractical aspects of the runway. Makeup consultants are also practical resources for finding the best products for your skin type in terms of foundations, powder, eye shadows and more.

Be willing to let them know what your budget is, so they can help you find the best products in your price point. You will be surprised at the amount of quality options available. Also, keep in mind, with better quality products, a little often goes a long way. Don't be unwilling to splurge a little for quality and better ingredients. After all, we fed your insides but we need to make sure we are taking the same care with your outsides.

| **Pin-Up:** Feeling Beautiful |

Think stylish versus trends. Stylish pieces have longevity. They are typically well made and fit us correctly. We feel beautiful and sexy in these pieces. The best part is that we can completely change the look by changing the accessories or even just swapping a few pieces in and out of a look or outfit. Designers create what is referred to as a "look" book. This book documents multiple ways that you can wear various pieces, stretching a 20-piece wardrobe into a well over 2 dozen or more looks. Think of your wardrobe. Do you have those staple pieces or are they all trends of the moment that are no longer "in"? When you chase the trends, you spend a lot of money for looks that may not be flattering to your body type or your coloring.

I want to make this clear. Fashion is about what works for you, not your next-door neighbor or your best friend. You need to enjoy dressing yourself and feel beautiful every day with your fashion choices. Of course, this all comes back to knowing yourself and what works best for your frame. I know a gentleman who is very broad in the shoulders, but thinner at the waist. His problem with jeans is finding ones that give him enough room in the thighs. Belts are always a necessity, because getting them big enough for his thighs generally means going one or two waist sizes higher. Can you relate to his struggle?

We all have that one area that always needs to be our first consideration when choosing clothing. It is a reality that we cannot ignore. To be truly comfortable in a piece of clothing, we need to be willing to tailor it to our bodies. It is the rare individual who can go to a rack of clothing and just grab something and look spectacular in it.

Therefore, you need to find a good tailor. The second thing is to recognize that those crazy fashions on the runway are not meant for real life. What looks great on those models was essentially custom created for them by the designers. So don't panic if you can't always meet the expectations of the trend. Instead, make the trends work for you. That could mean just taking a particular shade or using an accessory to compliment your outfit. The point is that the way you dress is about making you feel gorgeous.

As we age, it might seem that is harder to do. After all, parts are sagging, wrinkles are appearing and we are creaking more than ever. The aging process is not the same for everyone, but it also doesn't have to signal the end of our most beautiful selves. For men or women, the point is to find a way to stay cute, handsome or sexy, no matter what our age. There are so many options available for you in terms of makeup trends, clothing styles and even your accessories. The possibilities are endless, but you need to be willing to open your mind to the opportunities.

While it might seem nice that we are the same size as our kids, it doesn't mean we should be shopping in their closets. What works for them is not going to send the same message on a grown adult. If you run your own business, then you need to make sure that your look is timeless, classy and professional. Your kid's closet is not likely to provide those pieces, so just stay out!

Additionally, there is your mate. No matter how much we might want to say we dress for ourselves, the reality is that we want to be appealing and attractive for our mates. Are we taking the time for ourselves to make that happen? Fashion and makeup are meant to bring out our best selves, but if we spend all our time in sweats, then our mates can forget how beautiful and graceful we really are. Don't let it happen! Take the time to invest in yourself and I promise the results will be worth it!

| **Fashion:** Making the Outside Match the Inside |

Let's take a moment and talk about what you are on the inside. The choices of dress, make up and our general grooming are sending out a message to the rest of the world about who we are as individuals. It means that we are telling the world that we care and love ourselves or that we don't appreciate who we are, just by the way we dress and groom ourselves. Do you think of yourself as a god or goddess? Do you treat yourself that way or do you treat yourself more as a servant of a god or goddess? How do you treat others? Do they want to be around you or is your beautiful wrapping covering up uglier personal qualities?

I want to take a moment to focus on this because I believe we create the perspective that we then use to judge our circumstances. If we have a negative outlook, then our perspective of our experiences is likely to focus more on the negative than what may have gone well. As humans, we tend to look for the negative first and this can be detrimental to our relationships.

Part of being a compassionate and caring person means that we are caring and compassionate with ourselves. Take the time to spend a day at the spa. I promise you, a massage at the spa is worth every penny. Your body will thank you and your mind will appreciate the chance to relax and de-stress. If we don't make the time to take care of our minds and bodies, all the makeup and fashion in the world can't hide it. Our personal integrity is built around our moral principles and how we follow those. Stressing ourselves out can make it harder to stick to our personal guns when we need to. Others are going to attack us through a variety of methods. The point is to find a way to make it beyond those moments without losing our own internal compassion and ability to care for others.

Kindness and being mindful of others has become a huge focus on social media, as the political and social discussions seem to get even more heated. When you take the time to find your personal calm and centre yourself, it makes it easier to be kind to others. Being mindful of the moments when you are stressed and find ways to reach a calm place in your mind. There are plenty of ways to do so. Some individuals use daily meditation, exercise or yoga. Then there are those that focus on their spirituality as a way to reach their personal calm. When you do so, then you will find that your joy for life will increase and your insides will truly match your outside look. You can look beautiful and be appealing to others who recognize your amazing qualities, while still acknowledging that amazing outfit!

But you might be thinking to yourself, I have great taste and love spending time perfecting my look or trying different trends. However, I have champagne tastes on a beer budget. We'll discuss how to change that in the next chapter.

CHAPTER 3
VIP WEALTH

| **Chapter 3** - VIP Wealth |

From stock tips to investment opportunities, we are all looking for ways to increase our net worth or make our money work for us. In the long run, no one wakes up in the morning and says, "I want to be working and living paycheck to paycheck for the rest of my life." Retirement has become the carrot that we keep striving for, but too few of us are able to attain. Investments can be growing by leaps and bounds one week and then tank the next. Real estate was once the safe route to increasing your net worth, but the latest series of economic downturns has demonstrated that is no longer the case.

The question we have to ask ourselves is how can we increase our wealth strategically? It comes down to making smart decisions based on the changing markets and keeping a certain amount of our wealth portable. Let's start by covering some key tips to building your personal wealth for the long term.

| **Diamonds:** A Girl or Guy's Best Friend |

When we think of diamonds, there is an immediate association with jewelry, particularly the type that goes along with romance and marriage. Investors have seen their timeless appeal and are looking to cash in. This commodity investment has the potential to have high returns. Their stability in the face of other normally secure investments has seen their popularity increase. The wealthy have been turning to hard assets; because they can enjoy them, while at the same time, hold on to them as their value increases.

Diamonds, on the other hand, are not just an investment to enjoy. They can also be a pure investment, with an increasing number of companies emerging with plans that replicate the gold and silver marketplaces, allowing for the development of diamond-backed trading exchanges or funds. However, there are issues with these funds, including difficulty in pricing diamonds and tracking those prices. Additionally, diamonds have boom and bust cycles as does anything else on the equity market. Gold and silver prices are more established, but the possibility for diamonds to have the same type of consistent value is still in the future.

Although these types of funds await SEC approval, diamonds still have value in terms of the supply and demand. This means that there are simply not enough mines producing diamonds to meet the demands of the consuming public.

However, at the moment, the only way to enjoy this type of investment is by purchasing individual stones and then holding on to them.

Auctions are a great way to both buy and sell diamonds, those that are rough as well as polished gems. Competitive bidding seems to be driving up the prices of diamonds. This is an investment that seems to be on an upward swing. Supply and demand are not the only drivers in this market. Every time a diamond changes hands, the price is marked up. If you receive the diamond directly from the polisher, for example, it is considered first hand. There are four principles of diamond investing, price transparency, quality assurance, costs of transactions and liquidity. Each of these can have an impact on your purchase and the value of your investment.

However, they are just one example of portable wealth. It is important to look for investments that can be quickly turned into cash, as well as investments that may take longer to liquidate. This will allow you to access assets during emergencies or changing circumstances, including natural disasters or other events. Therefore, your family will be cared for, regardless of the circumstances.

Part of the reason that you need to have a diverse investment portfolio is illustrated by such key economic moments as the recession of 2008 and the stock market crash of 1929. Both had huge impacts on the wealth of individuals and families. Many who had invested heavily in the stock market found themselves without anything to provide even the most basic needs for their families. Their wealth and resources were not portable, but were essentially just on paper.

How are your resources divided? Are they portable or all on paper? There can be financial upheavals at any time and it is key to have wealth that can be accessed as needed. This takes me to the point of intelligent investing. It is about more than just choosing the right stocks, but making sure that you have variety within your portfolio. Doing so means looking at investments for their short and long term potential. There will be plenty of irresistible offers, which might seem too good to be true. If they sound that way, they probably are.

Be sure that you do your homework and asking questions. Your money needs to work for you, but there is no reason to give it away! The point is to make sure that your agreements are bringing value to your portfolio. Working with an investment professional can be a good way to find the investments and funds that fit your financial plan and expectations.

| Pay Yourself First! |

We all have worked in some form of job that got us a paycheck. How did you spend yours? If you are like so many of us, you paid the bills and hoped there was something left over at the end to spend on a fun activity or splurge shopping. Now the question is, did you pay yourself? To build your net worth, it is key that you make your personal savings a priority. When you get paid, the first bill you need to pay is yourself. This means putting a portion of your check into savings. This personal nest egg needs to grow first to cover roughly six months of your expenses, which would include basics like rent, utilities and any other debt obligations you may have.

Once you reach that six-month threshold, you now have the ability to start investing. There are a variety of options available. Your risk level will play a factor in what you choose to invest in first. After all, a good rule of thumb is to not invest more than you can afford to lose, at least initially. However, as your nest egg grows, you may be willing to take greater risks for the potentially greater rewards.

Most employers, especially that offer a retirement fund, will also allow you to invest a portion of your wages into the fund. When you are in your twenties, retirement seems as far away as the moon from the sun. It might seem that you have all the time in the world, when in reality, every year that you aren't saving means that you are losing money. The important thing is to start saving early.

As part of your retirement fund, if you have the option, choose to invest your funds into the highest returning option possible. This also may be a higher risk fund. If you are closer to retirement, then consider a balance of risk. Your retirement planner can help you to find the balance that works for you. Depending on where you are from, you might receive a tax benefit for your retirement savings, so take advantage of that as well.

The reality is that there are plenty of areas where you need to pay yourself first. Another area is by improving your credit rating through on-time bill payments and reducing your debt. How does this pay you first?

- First, on-time bill payment means that you are paying less in late fees and added interest. Essentially, paying on-time saves you money!
- Second, reducing debt loads will reduce the amount of interest you will pay over the life of the debt. This is money back in your pocket.
- Third, reducing debt means that you are reducing your monthly obligations. This means your emergency fund can stretch farther because you have less expenses to cover on a monthly basis.

Clearly, it is important to pay yourself first, because it can have the greatest impact on your future in terms of what you have for an emergency, retirement and everything in between. To reach prosperity in your life, you need to make sure that you have paid yourself first to increase your ability to live the life you want to live later.

| Develop Deep Pockets! |

In order to develop deep pockets, you need to have more income than just a traditional job. This means potentially owning your own business, making passive income through real estate and other investments or even buying bonds.

Treasury bonds are offered by various countries and are essentially a loan that you are making to that country in exchange for a predetermined interest rate. It means that you will receive that rate of return no matter what else happens. These returns are typically not very high, but they can be counted on as a solid investment. However, you are not likely to see major growth in your nest egg with a large amount of these bonds.

The stock market does not guarantee returns, but the ability to see greater returns is there. This is where you need to determine the type of investments you want to make. The market is constantly in flux, no matter where you are in the world. Therefore, it can seem as if you are making and losing money on a daily basis. The first gut response is usually to buy or sell based on that day's market. When you do this, you are more likely to lose money in the long run. For many stock market investors, it is important to take a long-term approach to investing.

Buy stocks in companies that have shown that they can do well consistently over a period of time. Then hold those stocks. The result will be consistent dividends and you are likely to see a better return over the long run. Does that mean that you are going to always make money? No, there will be times when these companies see losses and as a stakeholder, you will too. You may also find that fundamental changes in various industries will mean it is time to sell some stock, and you may be selling at a loss.

The important point to note is that there is risk with investing in the stock market and you have to be prepared for potential losses. At the same time, with smart investing, you can make a profit over the long term. Here are a few terms that you will want to know as you start your journey into investing. Leverage – This is the use of various financial instruments or borrowed capital to increase the potential return of an investment. Businesses can also use leverage to finance a firm's assets. A firm with more debt than equity is considered highly leveraged.

Leveraged ETF (Leveraged Exchange-Traded Funds) – This is a fund that uses financial derivatives and debt to amplify the returns of an underlying index. Leveraged ETFs are available for most indexes, including the Nasdaq 100. These funds aim to keep a constant amount of leverage during the investment time frame, such as 2:1 or 3:1 ratio.

Residual Revenue – This is money made over and above an initial sale, with little additional work, that typically pays out on a predetermined schedule. This would most likely refer to investment earnings from stocks or royalty income from intellectual property.

Passive Income – This type of income is received on a regular basis, with little effort to maintain the income stream. The American Internal Revenue Service defines rental income and income from "trade or business activities in which you do not materially participate," as passive income.

I also want to touch on investing in a business outside of the stock market. There will be individuals who own a business and are looking for capital to make a major purchase or to upgrade technology to help their business grow. Others may be looking for startup capital to get their business off the ground and the doors open. Whatever the case, you as an investor need to look past the sales pitch and ask the hard questions, both about the industry, potential competition, the product and the costs associated with production, sales and general overhead. You also need to know how much of a voice you have in the business once you invest. Some agreements will give you a vote and others will make you a silent partner that makes you unable to make decisions when you see the business taking a negative turn.

If you don't feel your questions are being answered fully or your gut instinct is telling you that the risk level is too high, then you need to walk away. Another investment will come along, but you have to remember that you are in charge of your bottom line. Choose investments that will allow you to reach your long term financial goals. Financial planners can provide the guidance you need to choose your goals and outline the steps to reach them.

Retirement can be less stressful if you know that you will have income long after you stop doing your daily commute. It's important to tap the right resources that will allow you to grow your net worth and give you the abundance you need to reach your goals. It is more than just budgeting, but it involves have a long-term view of your finances and your goals.

Just remember that every investment is a potential opportunity for a great return or a loss. By doing your research and making sure that you have all the facts available, you can make the best decisions to minimize your risk and potential loss. Investing is a science of sorts, but with the ability to learn and understand how to grow your money affectively, you can invest with the ability to grow your capital and overall fortune.

| Starting a Business |

A vast majority of millionaires and billionaires are business owners. It is a key to growing your wealth by owning a piece of the action, instead of being a clog in the wheel of a business. The question is what type of business that you would like to be involved in? What sparks your passion? Once you decide, then it's time to explore the options available to you.

Business options abound, but I can tell you from experience, that owning a business is not easy. When you add a traditional brick and mortar location, you have the added overhead costs that come with a physical location. At the same time, it is a presence that can draw potential customers to your business.

Online businesses have exploded because they have significantly less overhead and are open 24 hours a day, 7 days a week. You are earning money even when you are sleeping or involved in other activities. Digital products are also easier to deliver and typically cost much less to produce. In reality, this can often be the best way to start a business with minimal upfront costs.

Keep in mind, however, that any business will require a significant commitment of time and effort before it can become less hands on.

Overtime, online business opportunities can be a viable option. The point is that you have to decide what you want to commit to it, including the amount of time and other resources. Done For Your business options or affiliate marketing could be the way to start a business, because it usually has a system that you purchase and follow, versus reinventing the wheel again. If you choose to own business, be sure that you have an exit strategy, including when you would be selling the business and the amount you want to receive for it. Then you can build the business to reach that net worth and meet your long-term exit strategy.

As you grow your capital, you are putting yourself in a position to afford the lifestyle that you want to live. This includes the type of traveling you want to do, volunteering or even hobbies that you want to pursue. If you don't make the right financial choices, you will find yourself in the position of not being able to pursue your dreams, but always struggling to care for your long-term expenses. The point is not to work until you drop at your job, but to enjoy your life to the fullest, in a truly VIP style.

We have discussed how to turn your finances into VIP wealth, but now we'll talk about a skill that is necessary for every entrepreneur or business owner.

CHAPTER 4
VIP SPEAKING

| **Chapter 4** - VIP Speaking |

From the beginning of our educations, we are all taught how to stand in front of others and present an idea or defend a belief. Depending on your school, the presentations could have been more in depth in terms of research or they were short and sweet, making just a few key points. A few of us can still remember our first case of nerves and stage fright as we stood up in front of our peers to talk. I can remember being sure that I would forget everything and be the talk of the school forever! Teenager extremes aside, we survived those initial speaking attempts and may have thought that our speaking engagements were over once we left school. But your line of work or career may have changed that.

Today, professionals need to not only be able to give a presentation, but sell themselves, their point of view and their product. You need to become a storyteller that draws your audience in and brings them onto your side. Let's talk about some ways to keep your audience fascinated and curious throughout your presentation or sales call.

| **Drama is in the Details!** |

Have you ever had a conversation with someone who you just met and they tell you all the details of your life in just the first few minutes of your conversation? Is there anything that will compel you to keep the conversation going after that first few minutes? Probably not. The reason is that there is no mystery or drama left. You don't have the fun of learning about someone through a natural back and forth exchange. Additionally, they were so focused on telling you about themselves that they didn't even think to ask key questions to draw you into the conversation.

This example demonstrates how you need to be flexible when dealing with customers or in a professional environment. Your audience needs to be drawn into your presentation. So don't give them all the details at once. Tell a story and give the details as needed. Your audience will follow your lead. At the same time, they still want to know the reason for your presentation. Make it clear, but don't hesitate to weave your theme into your story.

When you start your presentation, you are already aware of where you are going and where you hope to end up in terms of motivating your audience to action. The audience is not in the same position. They have no idea where you are headed. Make your presentation one that keeps their attention and allows them to make the leaps of logic where you need them to and leaves them motivated to take action.

Susan, I want to have these kinds of presentations, but I have a horrible time when I stand in front of audience. What can I do to make it better?
Watch the Masters – When you are trying to create a successful presentation, it can be helpful to look at other successful speakers. Tapes are available of a variety of speakers, including Winston Churchill and other leaders. Note what styles and habits they demonstrate and then use them to inspire your own presentations and speeches.

Present Yourself Well Before You Speak – It might seem to be a no-brainer, but it is key to make sure that you look as professional as the situation requires. The better you look, the more ready and professional you will feel. A lot of people are going to be looking at you, so you need to make sure that you look the best you can. This is especially true if you are giving a sales presentation, because you are representing not only yourself, but also your company or business.

Familiarize Yourself with the Environment – When you are speaking in a new environment, take the time to get familiar with the size of the space and the acoustics. Determine how loud you need to be for your whole audience to hear you effectively. If you are going to be using a microphone, test it beforehand. The point is to make sure that you can be heard effectively; otherwise you won't be able to truly reach your audience and move them to action.

Avoid Liquid Courage – If you are speaking at a social function, and then avoid the temptation to partake of some liquid courage before you speak. Listening to a sincere speech from someone who is nervous is better than listening to someone who doesn't make any sense because they are intoxicated.

Know Your Subject – When you are making a presentation, it is important to be familiar with your topic. There are speakers who prefer to wing it, but doing so puts you in the position of being caught off guard and looking foolish in front of your audience. While you should be flexible and go with the flow of the discussion, it is critical to know your topic and the points you want to cover. The better you understand your topic, the more confident you will be when you stand in front of others to discuss it.

Practice Makes Confident – Once you have your presentation points in mind and your notes written out, then practice your speech multiple times until you feel familiar with the topic and your main points.

However, avoid the temptation to memorize your speech, because if someone asks a question that you aren't expecting, it will throw you off. Instead, use the main points to extemporarily speak on your topic, but make sure you are familiar with them by practicing.

Visualize Success – If you think you aren't going to give a successful presentation, then you are likely predicating what will happen. However, if you visualize yourself giving a successful presentation, then you will likely have that outcome. The point is to build your confidence by seeing a successful outcome. Negative thinking sets your brain to achieve a negative outcome.

Who's Your Audience? – Depending on who your audience is, your speech or presentation may need to change. For example, if you are speaking to colleagues, then you are not necessarily going to have to define industry terms. On the other hand, if your audience is less familiar with those industry terms, then you need to be sure that you explain or define these terms for them. If you don't, you will find that your audience will be lost and unlikely to follow your presentation. Tailor your speech and its delivery to meet your audience's needs and expectations.

Take a Deep Breath – The reality is that we are often our own worst critic. However, if you miss a sentence in your notes, it is not as if your audience will know. If you make a mistake or move past an image too quickly, just take a deep breath. It is a speech and everyone makes a mistake from time to time. A hiccup is not likely to cost you your audience's attention or their motivation to take action. Still, if you dwell on it, you are likely to make more and that can impact your audience's reaction. So breathe and then move forward.

You Might Be Nervous, But Don't Say So! – Your speech will have a lot more weight with your audience if they don't know you are nervous. Don't show the cracks in your armor. Instead, be confident, even if you don't feel that way. Doing so will help you to stay in control of your presentation, instead of appearing as if you don't really know or understand your topic.

Don't Race Through – When you are writing a speech, you might be thinking quickly. But when it is time to deliver that speech, you need to slow down and make sure that your audience has time to absorb what you are saying. Lightning fast speaking makes it hard for your audience to follow you, but at the same time, it shows your audience you are nervous. During your practice sessions, make sure that you are speaking slightly slower than your normal tempo.

Eye-to-Eye – When you try to connect with your audience, it is important to remember to speak to them, not the floor. Your confidence is apparent when your head is up. Plus, it puts your audience at ease and allows you to adjust the tempo of your speech to keep your audience's attention. Additionally, eye contact can help you to see if you need to explain something in greater detail, because you will be able to see and gauge your audience's reaction. Remember your presentation is an interactive one and so you need to be aware of your audience's reaction to maintain your command over the room.

Break the Tension with a Laugh – While your topic does dictate how serious you need to be, at the same time a few light hearted comments can often help to keep your audience engaged and connected. A well-timed joke can often win your audience over, even before you get into your topic. They will see you as human, which can be a plus. Still, you don't want to overdo it, as your audience might take your presentation less seriously. The rule of thumb: Keep it light when the material calls for it, but be serious when the material demands it.

Acknowledge Mistakes – If you have made a mistake during your speech and it is an obvious one, acknowledge it and then move on. Don't dwell on it and your audience will soon forget about it as well. However, when I say move on, I mean that you should not remain fixated on it. Your audience will forget quicker if you don't bring it up repeatedly.

Short and Sweet – No matter how much information you may have to present, the reality is that your audience can only absorb so much. As a result, you will want to make sure that you aren't the speaker that your audience remembers only because they kept going forever. Remember, they don't need every detail right now. Create some mystery, because that will keep your audience engaged. When you are at a sales call, keeping your speech short and sweet will allow you to engage with your client and leave them with an expectation of more at future meetings.

Audience is King/Queen – When you are preparing to give a speech, it can be easy to focus on you and how you feel about what you are presenting. The reality is that it isn't about you, it is about motivating your audience to act or imparting critical information. Concentrate on the message, not on telling your life story. Make it engaging, but remember, you are not the focus for your audience, merely the vessel bringing them the information that they need to act. Keep your objectives in front of you, and don't get so wrapped up in your own personal details.

Fake Confidence and It Will Come – There are plenty of days when it can be difficult to be or feel confident. We might have had a million things go wrong. In those moments, the key is to fake a high confidence level. Why? Because our brains are trained to make a reality based on perceptions or how we behave. When we act confident, our brains react as if we are confident. Eventually, our confidence becomes a reality. But until then, fake it. After a while, you will feel comfortable and confident for real. In the meantime, your audience is unlikely to know the difference.

You Are the Best You – In the end, you have your own unique flair that will come through with any presentation. Therefore, it is key to remember that unique spark and let it shine during your performance. Are you going to connect with all the members of your audience every time? It is not likely, but your personality will make a connection with someone. Additionally, the audience wants to see you succeed, so be the best you possible and let the audience do their part.

| Focus on the Audience |

Now that we have talked about all the ways that you can make your presentation better, it is time to focus on how to make a connection with your audience. Ask yourself these key questions:

1. What is my subject matter? Is it interesting or does it tend to be rather dry? How do I spice it up if necessary?
2. How can I make this topic interesting to my audience?
3. If I am in doubt about what the audience needs to know, have I asked them?

When you stop and think about the needs of your audience, you are going to find a way to meet those needs in your speech. Let's think about those industry professionals again. Do you really need to cover basic concepts with them? If not, then skip those and get to the meat of the discussion. Give them what they want. Throughout the presentation, observe your audience. Are they responding to you with head nods or other facial expressions that indicate they understand what you are talking about? Or do they look lost and confused?

Taking the time to check in with your audience, through eye contact or checking their facial expressions and body language, will allow you to make those critical adjustments to your presentation to make it more palatable to them. This means stopping to expand on points when necessary or skipping past or shortening areas of your presentation where you can see your audience is growing bored and losing interest.

Many speeches and presentations are trying to give your audience something specific. One reason could be to share knowledge or assist in teaching them to complete a new task or learn a new system. It could also be a way to empower your employees or co-workers by keeping them up to date with changes happening within the organization.

Presentations can also be about training or developing your workforce. Teachers and other professions are often required to complete continuing education and prove their attendance. If your presentation is providing that for your audience, ask questions and engage them with the material. This will help them later to recall key points.

Mentoring and facilitating change can also be part of any presentation. You are working with your audience to create a connection that will move them to complete a task, take on more responsibility or just accept a larger change within the organizational structure. Your presentation may be more about helping them to feel secure in their job during a major restructuring. The point is to connect with your audience, so they can take your information in without resistance.

Your presentation should always cover these main points:

- Tell the audience what you are going to talk about.
- Show them visually what you need them to understand, if possible.
- Let them attempt a task as part of your presentation, if possible. If not, describe the task with plenty of detail and be open to questions.
- If possible, let them complete the task successfully under your supervision. That may mean that they have a couple of opportunities to try as part of your presentation. After all, hands on is an extremely affective teaching tool.

As the presenter, it is important that your audience feel that you are invested in their success as well. Be interested in the question you receive and if you already covered the information, just rephrase for your audience. It is possible that your original explanation went by too quickly for them or then just need to hear it in a different way to digest it properly. The point is that you need to connect with your audience, even on a deep level.

That connection comes when your audience can feel that you are invested in them. Show that you relate to them and their current needs. Build a rapport throughout your presentation. This can include illustrations that they can relate to or even a few laughs. If you work more closely with members of your audience, you want your presentation to strengthen those relationships and help you to draw even closer as a team.

Have you ever seen an affective sales pitch? What made it a successful sales pitch? Here are just a few of the ways that it is affective.

- Make Irresistible Offers – No matter who is making the sales pitch, the audience needs to find the offer irresistible. They need to see it as the answer to a problem or obstacle that they simply cannot do without. This will help to compel them to act to meet that need by connecting with you and taking advantage of what your product or service has to offer.

- Create Compelling Value Propositions – As the presenter, it is key to make sure that your audience sees value in what you are presenting and in what you are asking them to do. When they feel the connection of value and how it can positively impact them, they will be more likely to act. At the same time, if they can't see the value in your product or services after your presentation, they are less likely to decide to work with your company.

- Create a Sense of Urgency – Deadlines are compelling for a reason. They create a sense of urgency and a willingness to move someone to do something they might not have otherwise done. As a presenter, it is up to you to create that sense of urgency for your clients or audience. Make them see why waiting could be costly to them in the short and long run. Doing so will create powerful motivation.

- Generate a Call to Action – Now that you have motivated them to do something, you need to tell them what to do. After all, you are the one in command at this point and you need to provide them with an actionable road map to achieve the desired result.

Now that the presentation is over and you have connected with your audience, you need to maintain that connection, especially if you are working with a client to complete a sale. That means following up with the client to make sure they have no further questions. It could also mean that you need to be persistent with your client, so they continue to feel the urgency from your original speech or presentation. This would involve maintaining regular and consistent contact.

When they communicate with you, are you quick to get back with them or do you leave them hanging for days at a time? That lack of attention can keep you from making that final sale or closing the deal. Therefore, it is key to be available after the presentation is over. Keep asking questions to find out what else they might need to know and don't forget to ask them to make a purchase or, if they have already made a purchase, ask them for referrals.

When working with referrals from your clients, make sure that your presentations can address any misinformation that they may have. After all, your client passed information on about your products and services, but like a game of telephone, the information is not always relayed 100% accurately. Or what they were told may have confused them or raised questions about how it can impact their business. Therefore, take the time to explain key concepts and ask questions to gauge their level of understanding before you proceed with your presentation.

| Make It Effective |

To have a presentation give the right impression, there are a few points that you need to keep in mind. Avoid using words, such as "um", "and uh" or "like". These can make you seem unprofessional and as if you do not know your subject.

Be sure that you take moments to pause throughout your presentation, so your audience has a chance to digest what you have to say. Have a question and answer period if time permits. Doing so will allow you to address areas that may be confusing your audience or that they found unclear. Don't cram so much information into your presentation that your audience is overwhelmed. Choose your key points to convey the message of your brand without creating an overload for the key members of the audience.

The point is to grow your business and make progress by use of affective presentations. Throughout my book, it is clear that you need to be proactive to connect with yourself, but also your audiences. If you would like assistance to take your presentations and speaking skills to the next level, contact me through my website, **www.gotTHEpowers.com**. I would love to work with you and help you to achieve your goals by reaching your audience affectively!

Before you head out to that presentation, take a look in the mirror. If you can identify the decade when everything in your outfit was in style, it's time to consider turning yourself over to the professionals! Stylists can be a great tool in anyone's pocket when it comes to changing, upgrading or revamping your look, as we will see in the next chapter.

CHAPTER 5
VIP SHOPPING

| **Chapter 5** - VIP Shopping |

Have you ever wondered what it would be like to tell someone else what you want and then just have the product show up at your home? The beauty of delegating your shopping to a professional is that you are able to get what you want without the hassle of doing it yourself. Still, there are some of us who just love browsing the shelves and racks to find that perfect item. No matter how you prefer to do it, the reality is that shopping is part of our lives.

However, there are ways to make it a more enjoyable experience. One such way is to delegate your needs to someone who makes it their career. Yes, I am talking about hiring a professional, such as myself, to assist you in creating your look and taking the hassle of shopping off your hands. Let's discuss how!

| **Delegate to a Professional** |

When you are working on defining your style or taking your taste to the next level, a stylist is key to making your shopping experience everything that it can be. A professional can assist you in finding the best pieces to fit your body and the message that you want to send to the world. Keep in mind that a good stylist will ask you questions about your taste, getting to know you as a person.

Not all of us are presenting the image that we want to. Maybe we had a new baby and you are feeling frumpy or just out of sync with dressing your new body. Perhaps aging has brought you to the point that your look is out of step with where you are in life now. For all these reasons and many more, a professional stylist is key to getting back a feeling of being gorgeous, sexy and putting your best self forward.

Not all of us are looking to revamp our image, but some of us are looking to create a new image. This might be true if you are leaving college and entering the professional workforce for the first time. What is involved in creating your image? You need to know what styles will compliment your body, but also the types of accessories that will work best. Here is a great example of accessories working for you versus against you. Take big, chunky necklaces. There are some individuals who can be overwhelmed by a chunky necklace and other who pull it off with ease.

Do you know where you fall in that spectrum? The problem is that many of us shop without a clue about the type of accessories and clothing works best for us. We try pieces on individually, without determining how they will look as part of a complete outfit or what type of message that will send about us to others. Our careers are a key part of who we are, but if we are dressing against the code of our industry, we may find that we are setting ourselves back and making it harder for individuals to trust us in our new role.

What type of business are you going into? The industry can also dictate the clothing and accessory choices that you will be making. A stylist can ask key questions about what you do throughout the day, even down to how you need to be able to move. For example, if you are sitting at a desk for a majority of the day, you might be able to wear slightly dressier options. However, if your job involves moving files or climbing in and out of a vehicle all day, you may need more flexible clothing options to accommodate all the additional movement and different environments you will be encountering.

These professionals are key to providing you the advice you need to find the best clothes and accessories to fit your body shape and size. They can help you to accent your best features and hide the ones that you aren't flattered by. Once those have been decided, the rest of your clothing choices will be much easier to determine.

A stylist can also help you to create your own personal look book. This book allows you to see a variety of options in terms of looks that you can create just from a few basic pieces. With a wardrobe of 20 pieces, you can create a number of outfits. They can also look like new with just a few key accessories. By taking the time to put together your outfits in advance, it can be easy to look put together for any occasion at a moment's notice.

A professional is also going to be able to assist you in navigating the myriad of shops and the variety of options available. When you go to the store yourself, it can often be overwhelming. A professional can assist you in maximizing your budget and creating a look that speaks to who you are as an individual and a professional. These looks could include a more casual approach to dressing or a more upscale version of you.

| Boutiques, Jewelers and Queues |

One of my favorite places to shop is various boutiques. These are shops that sell stylish clothing, jewelry and shoes, often with a smaller selection that may be geared toward a specific lifestyle or trend. The boutique lifestyle shops are part of an idea developed in Europe that focused a store on a specific lifestyle theme, such as an outdoorsy lifestyle. The result is a store that lacks traditional department divisions, but instead allows you to build an outfit or look from head to toe.

Many of these boutiques offer shoes, clothes and accessories. Some of these boutiques may also focus on handmade or unique options that give you a unique flair. Many of us love the idea of coming up with an outfit that no one else is going to have. When you shop the box stores, it is truly clothing for the masses, with limited choices but large quantities of the options available. Building a unique and one of a kind look requires you to know what you want and keep striving to achieve it. You need to be willing to ask your stylist for what you want and be willing to keep shopping until you find it.

If you can't negotiate for a look that you want, you will find it difficult to negotiate for anything else in your life. Many of my clients come to me with a half-formed idea of the message they want their look to convey. We shop for quite a while to find exactly what works for them. It can mean moving beyond the traditional shopping experience and diving into a gender specific store, such as a ladies or men's clothing store. These stores cater just to your specific gender, so that you can explore a variety of choices and styles. Another plus with these stores is that they may offer a tailor or other alterations, allowing you to leave with a piece that is uniquely fitted just to you.

Let me take a minute to discussing tailoring. I mentioned it previously in the Beauty chapter the importance of fit when it comes to your clothing. When you are at a boutique, it is clear that they take that to heart. The sales person will be looking at how you walk, stand and even sit in a particular piece of clothing. They will be looking to make sure that it is well fitted, but that you feel comfortable in it. Rule of thumb: If you don't like a piece or you don't feel comfortable, say something.

Your stylist can learn more about you if you speak up when trying on various items. Let them know who you are and why you don't feel right in a specific piece. Is it the cut, the color or the overall fit? By speaking up, you can make your voice heard and get what you need out of your experience with the stylist. At the same time, be willing to explore and try something new, before just shooting it down as not your style.

Getting out of your comfort zone in revamping your look is going to mean that you need to consider clothing options that you might not normally choose. The results can mean that you find the perfect clothing for your new look and a new favorite outfit. Reaching beyond what you always pull out of your closet can give you a sense of the possibilities that are available. It is also a chance to learn what you didn't know about fashion. Perhaps you have been living by outdated myths. Let your stylist help you to break away from those myths. There are possibilities that you might never have considered that may end up looking fabulous on you!

It isn't always easy to try something new and break out of what you are used to, but the results can be worth all the effort that you put into it. However, it is important to decide that you are worth all the effort and require this type of pampering.

Jewelers are also a necessary resource. Costume jewelry is fun and a great way to change up your look. But for the quality and timeless pieces, you need to find a jeweler. They can provide you with amazing pieces that will compliment a variety of looks. Women and men both need to know a quality jeweler. Accessories are not limited to one gender or another. However, they can finish off your look and make it truly polished.

Still, you might be thinking, jewelers are expensive and out of my budget. Before you dismiss them out of hand, remember, it is possible to find beautiful pieces for every budget. You can find the right fit your style and to match the message you want to put out in the world.

When it comes to queues, let's face it. We all hate standing in them and we prefer it even less when we have already spent the day trying on multiple outfits. When you work with a professional, you give them to power to take care of the queue for you. Depending on the personal shopper, you can create an account or find multiple other options to pay for the items they find on your behalf. The point is to take their professional services and use them to create the look that reflects where you are in your life or where you are headed. The possibilities are endless, but only if you are open to them.

A special note to the men reading this book: You need to take advantage of a stylist. Women shop frequently, but many of you men hit the discount store and buy pants, shirts, underwear and socks in bulk. If you are running your own business or looking to move up in your company, it is important to consider your look and clothes in bulk are not going to cut it.

Stylists are more than just a clothing purchaser; they are the ones that can put together a look based on you! It will be the message that you present to the world and you can't make it half-hazard or confusing. Be clear about who you are and be willing to use a stylist to assist you to convey that message effectively!

Now that you are ready to put that professional style forward, it's time to focus on how to grow your business through sales.

CHAPTER 6
VIP SALES

| **Chapter 6** - VIP Sales |

At the heart of any business are sales. If we do not have sales, we are not generating the income necessary to cover our business overhead and therefore, we are out of business. Customers, however, are not likely to just buy your product out of pity or to keep you in business. They must have a need that your product meets and then you must meet that need within their budget, while still making a profit.

Most of us are not born sales people. In fact, we might struggle to close the deal in a variety of areas of our lives. When we don't feel confident about our sales ability, we actually can make it harder to complete those sales and reach our sales goals. The importance of sales is more than just reaching an arbitrary sales goal. Making sales increases our income and can assist you to reach those financial goals, especially if you are the owner of your own business. Let's talk about how to turn your sales from average to VIP!

| **Secret to Sales:** Defining Your Market and Brand |

When it comes to increasing the sales of your business or company, you need to remember that you are in the business of turning a "no" into a "yes"! Your customers don't necessarily know that they need your product or services. You need to help them see how they can solve a problem or obstacle in their lives through doing business with your company. Before you understand the problems and obstacles of your audience, you need to define who your audience truly is.

This means defining and researching your market. Who is your target customer or client? It is important to be as clear as possible about what characteristics and needs that they demonstrate. Once you have your target customer, determine where you are likely to be able to reach out to them. Are they found on social media or is television a better media to reach them?

Once you have defined your target market and done your research, you need to determine who is your competition. How are you different from them? What can you offer your target customer that gives additional value over your competition?

Online marketing has opened a new doorway to reach your target customer. No longer are you limited by geography. At the same time, traditional marketing was not able to target an audience through very specific details.

Instead, the marketing campaigns naturally had to be broader. The internet has changed that and in a dramatic fashion. Cookies allow advertisers to track the sites your audience visits and create ads to draw their attention when they visit their favorite websites.

Even email campaigns can be used to target past customers or those who may have visited your site, but not yet made a purchase. The point is that marketing today can be tailored to create an individualized and personal feel for your target client. Your target audience may also have a target geographical area as well. Think about it this way. If you are offering a product for professionals in the technological industry, you might tend to keep your online marketing targeted to a specific geographical area. You are not likely to spend funds on ads in cities and markets where tech companies are not likely to set up shop.

This brings me to the importance of strategy. No business has an infinite number of funds that they can dedicate to marketing on a variety of platforms. In fact, it is more likely that you have a fairly limited budget. Therefore, it is important to look for a strategy that fits your products or services, and puts out a message that reflects your brand in a favorable way.

I want to stop for a moment and talk about brand image here. When it comes to building a brand, the effort involved is tremendous. Every little interaction with your target market and others become part of your brand reputation. While it can take a long period of time to build a brand reputation, it can only take a few minutes or one badly timed interaction to do serious damage to that same brand.

Take a bar in a small working class town. The owner wanted to do something for veterans, so he stopped to help a homeless man, posting a video of the encounter. After he did so, he started collecting a large amount of money that was to be given to a charity with a veteran focus. Weeks later, he had raised approximately $20,000 and it had been discovered that the homeless man he had encountered was not a veteran.

Suddenly, social media was buzzing about how he had scammed the public. His responses were of a defensive nature, and most importantly, they were not kind. The public associated the negative comments with his bar's brand and he started losing money as a result. People didn't come in and those that did often felt his anger at the failing of his business. It took a major PR effort to restore the community's trust in him and his business.

Eventually, he was able to find a veteran's association that accepted the funds collected and he repaired his brand image. But it took months to set everything right, and during that time, he lost hundreds of thousands of dollars.

My point is that you need to be a proactive brand manager. Before you respond on social media, take a deep breath. Then acknowledge the complaint and ask to take the discussion off-line to address the issue and make amends. Doing so will keep your online image intact, while at the same time, addressing legitimate concerns. Even if they choose not to work it out with you, your calm responses and lack of an attack posture or defensive attitude will assist in keeping your brand image in the positive with your clients and target market. Your customer service needs to make your clients feel as if they are VIPs. It will keep them coming back time after time.

| What are Your Options? |

When it comes to selling a product or service, there are plenty of ways to go about it. Telesales is a tried and true method. It involves employees placing sales calls to potential customers based on a list. They may have a specific number of points or a script to follow during their calls. These sales people must also be trained on the products or services that they are selling, so that they can answer potential questions and assist in teaching clients about the benefits and value that they offer.

Calls can be monitored and then used to find weaknesses in either the sales pitch or the interactions with the potential clients themselves. The benefit of this monitoring is that it can allow you to make adjustments to your processes and procedures as needed. Once those changes have been implemented, then you need to make sure that the sales people are updated on them by means of regularly scheduled trainings.

Sounds like a lot of work for potentially minimal return, doesn't it? Your employees could be on the phone for hours with little success. Hundreds of calls later and you are no further along than when you started. Why? Because the details about the target market are minimal at best.

The internet is a great way to reach your target demographic, simply because you can build advertising that is personalized to your audience. The results can be incredible in terms of return on investment, but the more targeted you are, the more expensive the ads can be. Therefore, you need to set a realistic budget and then stick to it. Also, measure the number of clicks and the number of actual sales you receive from your online site. If your advertising is not affective, then you need to tweak it to encourage more clicks to your website.

Using a website designer can also help you to draw your target audience. When they reach your site, it should be easy for them to navigate, and the checkout process should be intuitive. There should also be staff available to answer questions and make sure that products are being shipped in a timely manner to fulfill orders. You also have to manage your online reputation. Reviews are a big part of sales and repeat customers are your best advertisement. However, an unhappy customer is likely to be louder than all the positive reviews, so try to meet their needs effectively. If they don't feel ignored, you are likely to win over a negative voice to your brand's side.

If you choose to use a direct marketing approach, hire a professional. When you do it yourself, you actually may make mistakes that cost you more than you anticipated. Be clear what your budget is, but allow the agency to do their job and measure the results. This can help you to tweak your advertising as needed.

Packing and distribution channels also need to be set up to make sure that sales are fulfilled promptly, regardless of where the sale was made. Part of having a successful sales team is making sure that you are managing your customers' expectations affectively. When they decide to go with your company, you need to be sure that you have under-promised and over-deliver.

Your support staff also has to recognize their role in terms of dealing with the customer after the sale is completed. Building a relationship with your customers involves your support staff meeting expectations time after time. When you are tracking your customers and meeting their expectations, then you can expect repeating sales.

To build a VIP sales force, you need to keep in mind your target customer and what their expectations are. Decide how you want to reach out to them and then make sure that you keep your message consistent. Doing so will move your business forward and assist you in reaching your sales goals!

CHAPTER 7
VIP READING

| **Chapter 7** - VIP Reading |

Reading is a fundamental skill. There is nothing you can do in this life without the ability to read and understand the message that others are sending. Still, not everyone is a natural born reader. In fact, for many of us, a love of reading came later in life, if it came at all. If you are one of those individuals who finds reading a chore, let me ask you to give it one more try. As you will see, there is much that can benefit you, just by picking up a book.

| **Choose Your Medium** |

When it comes to choosing a book these days, there are plenty of options available. For the more technological among us, e-books and the electronic readers have become a huge hit. They allow you to take a library with you wherever you go. From plane rides to the bus, you can easily switch from an exciting fictional novel to educational non-fiction. The ability to carry all that in your phone or a small tablet is an indication of how technology has even transformed reading. Now e-books offer connections to additional resources, such as the author's website, references and even videos. Translation is also less complicated. Instead of printing books in dozens of languages, publishers have the option of making it available in an e-book format with multiple languages available at the click of a button.

For those hardcore readers who still prefer the old school method, there are still plenty of paperbacks and hardbacks to be had in your local bookstore or through your favorite online book selling website. Publishing has adjusted to the desires of the reading public, so there is a medium to suit everyone.

What do you enjoy when you have to read something? Do you enjoy holding a hard copy or is the electronic option more your speed? Whatever you choose, it is key to pick up a book. There are so many genres to explore. These can include mysteries, real life crime, literature, romance and science fiction. There are novels that bleed genres together, using a historical setting for a mystery with romance between two or more of the characters. Worlds come alive through the pages of a well-written book, regardless of the format that you choose to read it in.

Writers also can impart knowledge about cultures, the human experience and history. When we read, it allows us to get a different perspective from our own. Our world expands because we can walk in another person's shoes for a while.

There are literally hundreds of examples of characters that continue to live on in our culture because they were so well drawn by their creators. Words have power and writers can impact our society with their use of this power.

Images on the covers can spark our imaginations, making us want to open that book. Libraries are a great place to explore books, checking out the covers and finding the books that spur your imagination and grab your attention. You can learn and share experiences on a budget. Books are able to transport you and take you outside of your own world and its challenges.

This book is meant to spur you to take action in your own life, creating a VIP

| Step Into the Publishing World |

For those who enjoy reading, writing can be a logical next step to share your own stories and creativity. J.K. Rowling has written a successful series based on her imagination. She created a whole world and although it took some time, she found a publisher that could see what she was building and support it. The result is one of the best all-time selling series and a movie series that has a tremendous fan base.

The publishing world picks and chooses the voices that are heard because they choose the writers to publish. In previous decades, publishers controlled what hit the shelves of your local bookstore and the format that you received it. Authors might only rate a paperback with minimal marketing, while another book rated a hardcover and a large marketing push.

Then technology turned the publishing world on its head. Today, writers can self-publish using various options available through different sites. In addition, they can choose the format that they want to be published in. Now their voice can be heard. Traditional publishers have come with specific restrictions or contract clauses, whereas publishing yourself doesn't have those same restrictions. However, self-publishing does not have the same marketing arm that traditional publishing houses offer.

As a result, there are more options available for writers, but the results can be very uneven in terms of their ability to reach their audience effectively. However, writers are finding that publishing houses no longer have the hold over whose voices are heard anymore. When you cruise through Amazon, for example, you can see a mix of books by authors with different publishing methods. The results are incredible.

As a reader, it is a buffet of experiences to sink into. Take the step to expand your world by choosing a new book to read. Fall in love with a character. It is amazing how a writer can reach their audience and touch their hearts and souls. Yet writers are artistic individuals and publishing houses have traditionally had the dollars and cents at heart.

When you enter your bookstore, you are meeting the combination of the publishing world and the artistic world of the writer. Bookstores are built to draw you in and make you want to stay a while. They have started specializing in different areas, providing snacks and coffee, as well as comfortable chairs. It is meant to be inviting, drawing you in to sit and read for hours. Take the time to explore these bookstores, especially if reading is not on your list of fun activities. You may be surprised how easily you can find your way into the world of reading and how much you can enjoy the journey.

Reading can change your perspective, especially your view of the world at large. Suddenly, you can find that you have more empathy for others than you may have even thought possible. Reading opens up worlds and takes you out of your comfort zone. Literature is built around the idea of creating a world and introducing you to it.

Cracking a book is more than just an exercising in learning a new skill or exploring a new culture. It is a passport to see the world from your favorite chair. Travel budgets can be small, but with libraries and sales at the bookstores, you can go anywhere for pennies on the dollar.

VIP reading is about opening your mind to reading and the possibilities that will be in front of you because you took the time to read. This leads me to my next topic, which is the benefits of having a lifetime love of learning.

CHAPTER 8
VIP LEARNING

| **Chapter 8** - VIP Reading |

Learning is a lifelong process. If we choose to stop learning, then we are putting ourselves into the position of stagnating and not growing towards our true purpose and fulfilling our passion. Continual learning is about searching out knowledge and then connecting it to what we already know. This helps us to shape our worldview beyond the confines of our everyday lives. Still, it can feel as if there is no time for us to learn and grow. It's true; we need to make continual learning a priority. If you do, then the benefits are worth the effort!

| **Gaining Life Skills** |

I want to talk with you for a moment about cooking. I have friends that are not good at cooking. In fact, if it weren't for takeout, they would probably starve. Yet, I venture that most of us agree basic cooking is a life skill. If you can't do it, then you are likely going to find yourself hungry, unless you can afford takeout or a chef, which most of us can't afford to do on a daily basis. So what do you do? You learn how to cook basic meals. You might never end up being a Gordon Ramsey or one of those other culinary wonders, but you aren't going to starve. In the process, you may find yourself motivated to learn more complicated dishes. You may even find that you enjoy it!

The point of this example is to illustrate that we all have the ability to learn life skills. If fact, there are many that we already have, including basic grooming, dressing ourselves and caring for our basic needs. But beyond that, there are life skills that we need to deal effectively with others. Many of them we picked up from our families, mentors and friends. As adults, new experiences give us new techniques that we can implement in other areas of our lives.

Building our skill sets is about developing ourselves personally, not just professionally. Personal development has the added benefit of helping us to reach goals and dreams that we have envisioned for ourselves. Our personal vision for our lives comes about because we don't allow ourselves to stop learning.

Our skills and experiences contribute to our values and what we hold as important to our lives and our personal growth. Values then shape our perceptions. If we aren't willing to examine these values and beliefs once in a while, then we will stagnate as individuals over time. Life is about growth and a VIP life is about actively pursuing that growth. We'll discuss one key area for new experiences when I discuss travel in Chapter 10. But for now, let's focus on the growth that you can achieve while staying closer to home.

| Education: Yes, You Can! |

To learn anything new, we need to pursue the knowledge. Decades ago, education was focused on leaving high school and obtaining a university or college degree. Now there are more options available for those who want to expand their education. This includes online schools, seminars, conferences and even self-learning.

What is self-learning? It is when you decide to let your curiosity lead you. Take advantage of the local library, classes at your local community college or even following a topic online. There are so many ways to find out more about multiple topics.

Training opportunities provided through your job and industry can also provide a way to expand your knowledge base. Take the time to grow beyond where you are in terms of skills and experience. When you do, you will be amazed at what you can accomplish.

Mentors and coaches are also a great way to increase your knowledge base. After all, a coach can teach you a specific set of skills. This can be a great way to expand professionally. However, a mentor can help you to design a set of goals and a path to reach them. Then a mentor can help to hold you accountable to reach those goals and stay on that path. The point is that education is not limited to what we can learn in a structured environment.

Degrees might seem impressive when you are applying for a job or moving up in your career, but it can ultimately be just a piece of paper. How are you applying what you have learned on a daily basis? Are you building upon your foundation of knowledge? Or are you making the decision that what you know now is good enough? When we limit ourselves, it impacts more than just us, but impacts our relationships as well.

The reality is that our lives are enriched when we expand our knowledge base, tying what we already know with new information. As we do, we expand our perceptions of the world and even make changes to our own values and beliefs. Wisdom is created when we see the connections of information and can use them in our lives to initiate impactful change for others and ourselves.

Our brains are made to grow and make more neurological connections. Research has shown time and time again that it is critical to continue to exercise our brains and make those new connections, because they can provide much needed protection for our brains from a variety of diseases. The more we learn and then put it into practice, the stronger we can make our brains over the long haul.

A VIP life is based on learning, growing, and experiencing new things that inspire us and help us become the best version of ourselves. When we examine how our brains function, it is clear that our self-talk can be influenced by what is happening around us. That means our viewpoint can be negative or positive depending on what we choose to surround ourselves with. When we are learning more about ourselves, other cultures and the larger world, we are putting ourselves in a position to be grateful. We can cultivate the necessary positivity to see the best in our lives.

At this point, we have to step back and talk about our confidence level. When you learn something new and you execute it, it is a confidence boost; there is no question about it. Executing new skills successful gives us another source of positive internal self-talk, which continues to boost our confidence. Understand that when you tell yourself it is possible and then deliver; you will believe it is even more likely the next time.

Without those positive experiences, your viewpoint of life can easily turn negative. Once it turns to a negative point of view, then it is hard to feel the desire to strive to learn and grow. Therefore, to have the greatest impact on your life, pick up a book, take a walk, sit through a seminar, or find a mentor, but do something that will broaden your horizons. A VIP life awaits when you open the door to another challenge!

CHAPTER 9
VIP MEETING

| **Chapter 9** - VIP Meeting |

As an entrepreneur or business owner, meetings with our employees and clients are a fact of life. Within these meetings, deals are made, ideas for marketing and products are formed and the course of your company is decided. Therefore, it is key that you become a VIP in terms of running and executing meetings effectively. Those who don't improve their skills in this regard are likely to find their meetings running them, instead of the other way around.

| **Brainstorming** |

Not every meeting is scheduled with a specific purpose in mind. There are just as many meetings meant to tap the creativity of the team in overcoming an obstacle or issue that the company leadership needs to address. Have you ever sat through a brainstorming session? At times, it can be almost chaotic, as everyone throws out ideas, some of them unrealistic or unworkable. In the end, out of all that chaotic noise, there gradually comes a few viable ideas that can be implemented.

It is those potential gems that drive brainstorming sessions. Hearing an idea can spark something for someone else and the possibilities are endless. However, to truly benefit from a brainstorming session, there need to be a few basic ground rules. These can help to keep the session from getting bogged down into unproductive discussions and keep the focus on the main challenge or obstacle at hand.

Everyone deserves to be heard. In brainstorming sessions, often the loudest voice gets heard, while everyone else gets drowned out. As the mediator of a brainstorming session, one of your jobs is to make sure that all voices get heard. Those quieter members of your team might be holding the answer to your challenge. How can you encourage everyone to contribute? Start your brainstorming session with a round robin, where everyone must contribute something in the first round. Accept all ideas, no matter how crazy they might seem at first. The point is to open up the possibilities, while breaking down assumptions about the problem's limits.

Why is it so important to hear all those voices? The quieter and more introverted members of your team might also be the most analytical. It means that while others are talking, they are taking in information and making assessments about what could be affective and what will not work. Often, they are also aware of the resources available. You want to hear what they have to say. Your loud and creative team members are key as well, because they bring great big ideas to the discussion. Still, without a balance, you might not be benefiting from all the strengths that your team has to offer. Brainstorming can help you to bring the diverse experience of your team into play as well.

Chair your team so that even those seemingly crazy ideas do not get crushed right away or dismissed out of turn as being unreasonable. Gather individuals from a wide range of disciplines within your organization, so you can get more input on how potential ideas could impact various departments as you brainstorm. The point is not to stifle creativity, but to gather as much information and various thought processes as possible.

Using a round robin approach, at least initially, will make sure that you give a voice to all. Once you have done a few round robins, start whittling down the ideas on the board. This could be the point where you discuss available resources, timing and man-hours needed to implement the idea. You may find that some ideas will fit better into your long-range strategy versus your short term one. This might mean that you don't move forward with it at the moment, but you don't abandon the idea either. However, at this stage, some ideas are going to hit the trash bin, even some of your own. Show your team that it isn't personal if you don't move forward with their idea by demonstrating the right attitude when you don't move forward with one of your own.

Have you found that your team works together but lacks a bond that takes their work to the next level? Brainstorming together can help to build that bond, while at the same time, building the team's commitment to the final solution. After all, if they helped to develop it in a fun environment, they will be more willing to work toward its success.

While it isn't necessarily a team vote to determine which ideas get moved on to research and assessing the costs of implementation, your team's enthusiasm will be sparked when they see you taking their opinions into account. It will help your team to feel invested in what they are working on and that enthusiasm will be beneficial as you move a project forward.

Here are steps to keep your brainstorming session at the VIP level:

Prepare the Group – Set up a comfortable meeting place and make sure that the room has all the tools and resources that you might need. Don't forget the snacks! If there is background information your team needs before the session, make sure that it is available.

Recognize that there is some freewheeling as part of the session, so don't make it all about the background information. That could stifle the creativity of your group as a whole. Make the group as diverse as possible, with various backgrounds and thinking styles. Appoint a recorder, but don't make it someone who you want to have contributing ideas, as it can be hard to record and contribute at the same time. Post notes where the group can see them and refer back as needed. Finally, as part of your prep, consider a warm up exercise to the get the team engaging with each other before you get started.

Present the Problem – Define the problem or challenge in a clear manner for the team. Lay out any necessary criteria that will need to be met. Make clear your objective is to get as many ideas as possible. Allow individuals a few minutes to jot down ideas of their own before opening the session up to group discussion. This will give you the ability to implement a round robin system more effectively.

Guide the Session – Use group discussions to develop key ideas further and to create potential new ideas. Discourage criticism or shooting down ideas with the phrase, "That won't work!" Instead, focus on generating ideas and boosting creativity. At this point, the practical and impractical ideas can dwell together. Time enough to separate them later. Avoid staying on one train of thought for too long, but switch gears frequently to generate a number of different approaches, as well as to explore individual ideas in more detail. Allow team members to tune out for short periods of time to explore an idea further as an individual. Break as frequently as needed to keep the group excited and engaged.

Once you have all these ideas or have narrowed it down to a few viable ones, it is important to assign individuals to explore the idea further, including implementation and costs. Doing so will help you to determine how viable a solution it is and at the same time, begin the process of moving that idea forward. Analyzing the ideas will help you to reach a viable solution with a plan of action. Brainstorming is truly an effective way to find the solution to any challenge facing your company or team.

| Vision Boards |

When it comes to moving an idea forward with your team, it can be hard to translate your vision in a way that motivates others. It is as if they can't see what you can see, so they have a hard time buying into your plan or idea.

A vision board is a great tool that can be used to clarify, concentrate and maintain a team's focus on the plan or idea.

The board can use combination pictures, words or phrases that inspire and assist your team to see where you want to go. A vision board can have several purposes, including:

- Identifying your vision and giving it clarity.
- Reinforcing your team mission.
- Keeping your attention on the goals at hand.

The beauty of technology is that these boards can now be created right on your phone, tablet or computer. That can put it in front of your team on a daily basis, reinforcing the ideas and goals that you want to keep them focused on. General goals can be made clear and given rich detail by means of a vision board. Suddenly, your team can see the idea as a tangible and achievable goal. They will see what you see and it can build a unity of purpose.

A vision board serves as a constant reminder to your team that this is where you are headed and keep them motivated to stay the course. It is amazing how a visual image of your goals can keep your mind focused and your attention on where you are headed.

The point of these methods is to keep your team moving forward and oriented on your goal. It doesn't matter if the end game is the implementation of a new process or system, but a vision board can assist your team to see the goal as achievable, especially when the process gets bogged down or issues arise that impede progress.

Momentum is also something that needs to be part of your team's efforts on a daily basis. It can be hard to keep your team's momentum on an upward swing when they are facing difficulties or aren't immediately seeing the successful conclusion of a project. Let's be realistic. Implementation is often a marathon, not a sprint. Your team's motivation needs to be there for the long haul, not the short term. Use vision boards to keep that motivation up, especially as you reach key milestones. Update the vision board and celebrate the successes. Your team will benefit from your efforts and your company will benefit by achieving key goals and milestones.

Personal vision boards are also important because you can use them to achieve personal goals as well. Envision the life that you want and use affirmations to help you to reach those goals.

| Check and Double Check: It's the Follow Up |

Finally, I want to talk about the follow up. Great systems and ideas can be implemented, but if you want to create a system, then you need to follow up. Check in with your team and gather feedback about the success so far and where there have been hiccups. Use contact reports to gather measurable information and feedback. Make corrections as needed and then gather more feedback. Creating a process and solving a problem are not going to happen overnight. You need your team to see that you aren't giving up, but are continuing to tweak to achieve better results.

At this point, you need to be clear about the type of results you are hoping to achieve and communicate those to your team. If they aren't sure what is expected, then the implementation might not be as effective as you hoped and could lead to the effort being abandoned altogether. Often, that can leave your team feeling deflated and less inclined to solve the challenge at hand.

How do you affectively measure results? First of all, choose what you want to measure. This doesn't mean create an exhaustive list, because that will quickly wear out both you and your team. Instead, choose key areas that can have a significant impact on the process or system. These will be areas that will show where the process is working affectively or not.

Another place to consider measurement is the cost and overhead incurred. Is the process or system paying for itself in terms of increasing efficiency or overall lowering costs? This could be a key area that decides if the system is working effectively or if changes need to be made. The reality is that many processes and systems are abandoned because they end up not being worth the investment in terms of their return.

However, if no risk is ever taken, then your team will stagnate, simply because they aren't moving forward in terms of new ideas, processes and systems. Technology is in a constant state of motion. No industry is able to ignore that fact. There may be implementation and change that needs to occur to keep up with your industry. While you might have meetings to get the ideas of your team, ultimately your executive team will be the ones to make the call and your team will have to accept the decision.

How do you keep them motivated when it is a major change that they aren't 100% behind?

Keep them informed. Take their feedback seriously. Share information whenever possible and be honest if you aren't able to give them more detail. Address rumors head on. Company culture comes into play here. If you have made your team a priority, then they will respond.

Additionally, help your team to feel invested in the process by implementing changes based on feedback where appropriate. The point of checking back in with your team is to see what is successful and what is not working. Continual improvement comes when you are revisiting and listening to your team. It creates a VIP environment, where you will get the best from your team and your company will benefit as a result.

CHAPTER 10
VIP TRAVEL

CHAPTER 10

| **Chapter 10 -** VIP Travel |

Traveling seems to be the realm of the wealthy and famous, at least if you look at the covers of various magazines in the line at the grocery store. But traveling is not an unattainable goal. In fact, technology has allowed us to experience more of our world than ever before. Travel websites have become even more user friendly, with prices that put a variety of travel options within the range of multiple budgets. Let's explore what you can find as you open your mind up to becoming global traveler.

| **Traveling the World** |

The world is literally full of hundreds of experiences, all waiting for you to come and enjoy them. If you love nature, there are nature preserves, national parks and a myriad of adventures you can have. Climb mountains, explore deserts, and even take the time to touch pieces of nature that have been around for hundreds of years.

Have you ever had the chance to dive beneath the oceans or lakes? The world under the water can be amazing, with the different creatures, plants and the ways that light filters through the waves. Getting the chance to observe these natural wonders can be an empowering and enlightening moment. Traveling also allows us to explore other cultures, learning about more than what is in our own neighborhood or unique walk of life.

Gaining a greater understanding of other cultures also has the added benefit of reminding us of our similarities as human beings. We are more than just a group of individuals, and it is imperative that we learn to work together with unity. Without a willingness to work together, our world can suffer much greater long-term consequences. History is riddled with examples of how governments and leaders used the differences between human beings to create divides that led to war and suffering with emotional and economic consequences for all involved. Europe itself has been a battle ground on more than one occasion.

Exploring other cultures also means deepening our understanding of history and the impact on our current world. There are many different opportunities to learn, grow and broaden our personal experiences in this world. Great, Susan, I want to do that, but how?

Budgets are a reality that a vast majority of us have to live with. How can you have the VIP travel adventures you crave, but on a limited budget?

First, start by signing up for various travel sites. There are plenty of package options that are available, if you are willing to take the time to look. Additionally, don't be afraid of the all-inclusive options. They can be a budget friendly way to package accommodations, food and even a few activities in one price. If you are more free-spirited or want to get a real feel for living somewhere outside of the traditional tourist areas, there are plenty of sites that offer bed and breakfast or even rental accommodations, but the pricing may be less than a standard hotel and provide a homier feel.

There are also plenty of sites that offer reasonable deals on travel in terms of planes and trains. While shopping these sites, be on the lookout for options that allow you to combine your car rental with your plane ticket. Often, these combos allow you to save a bit in both areas.

Travel is about shopping for the best deal. You may have to consider using a travel agent, who has access to packages that you might not be able to find on your own. Agents can also assist in dealing with paperwork and walk you through any steps you need to take before you leave your home country. A VIP traveler uses all the resources available to them.

Now I want to talk about airlines for a moment. These days it seems that a cheap flight means you get what you paid for. Those traveling in economy or coach find themselves with little in the way of food or drink options, little room and less entertainment options. Well that is unless you want to be nickeled and dimed to death by the airline. "What? Of course I would like to pay $10 for that little bag of pretzels and that flat soda! No pillows left? I will just bundle up my jacket and try to stay in my 24 inches of space, so I don't fall asleep on that man/woman next to me..." The list could go on and on.

While we can't change the airlines and most of us are not likely to want to pay for first class, there are ways to enjoy the amenities without the price tag. I am talking about upgrades. Most airlines offer miles that you can earn, both when you fly their airline and when you make purchases on a regular basis. Credit cards might also provide additional travel miles, although they may have different rules about what counts and how many you can earn in a specific period of time.

I don't believe in radically changing your shopping habits to capture all these miles, but you should be maximizing your normal everyday shopping to capture as many as possible. The reality is that when you do so, you are going to be able to earn those upgrades. Keep up with which airlines offer the best upgrades and how many miles you need to take advantage of them. Then set your goals and work for them.

If you fly frequently, then you should sign up for the frequent flier programs available on most airlines. They may charge a fee, but you may find that your upgrades are automatic as a result. They also offer their frequent fliers additional perks, such as a nice lobby to relax in, a place to change or shower and even an area to work or recharge your electronics. These perks are what make being a frequent flier worth the time it takes to sign up.

Another perk of these frequent flier programs is that they will often give you an automatic upgrade, once you have reached a certain number of flights or points. These upgrades allow the airlines to reward their regular customers and you want to be on that list. Where do you regularly fly from? What airlines use that airport as a hub? The airlines that fly out of your airport should definitely be the airlines you sign up with, but then don't hesitate to sign up for others, especially if your airport is small and you frequently have to take connecting flights.

I have found that it is worth it to create a spreadsheet with all your frequent flier accounts, their vital information and the credit cards or other payment options you have tied to the accounts. This will help you to keep organized. In addition, you can make a column for the number of miles you have and update it when you receive your statement from the airline. Of course, if you are planning a trip, check the airline's website to find out your most current mileage amount and what type of upgrades are available.

If you use discount sites, you might not always be able to use your mileage for an upgrade, so when you do want to use it, consider booking directly through the airline itself. The prices are often comparable, but this allows you to use your upgrades. Another note, consider using your upgrades on longer flights versus the shorter ones. The mileage amounts required can be large to receive a complete 1st class upgrade, so saving for them may take a few trips. If you use up the balance on shorter trips, then you might not be able to enjoy them when you really need them. Longer trips can be harder when you are in a smaller space in coach, so it is worth it to save upgrades and relax in style.

For example, a friend opted to fly to Hawaii 1st class. She went with a friend who had flown coach on a previous trip. Their experience was incredible. They boarded early, had more leg room, were fed multiple meals and even had a restroom that was for 1st class only. With plenty of pillows and blankets, it was a relaxing trip that left them ready to go when they landed. VIP rule of thumb: Long trips require 1st class. This rule applies particularly to international flights or ones that will be longer than 6 hours.

| International Travel |

When it comes to traveling internationally, there are more steps involved than a flight whose destination is within your own country. One of the first things to get is your passport. If you are traveling in the European Union, your passport is typically checked in your arrival country and then when you leave Europe. Still, a vast majority of countries view your passport as an international id card, with pertinent information about you. Each country's process for obtaining a passport is a little bit different, but most countries will take a few weeks, at minimum, to issue your hard copy passport.

Therefore, you will want to check your government's website and get those steps done early in your travel planning process for your first international trip. Once you have completed the process, be sure to do what is needed to keep it current, so you can enjoy the spontaneous international trip when the opportunity presents itself.

With that in mind, here are a few things to remember before you become a globe trotter. Much of this list is based on common sense, but the most important thing to remember is that you need to do your homework before you buy that ticket and start your adventure.

Health – The reality is that every country has slightly different diseases that you can be exposed to. Some of them you may have never even heard of before. Before you travel internationally, make sure that you are up to date on your vaccinations. Also, check to make sure that the country you are traveling to does not require any additional vaccinations. Depending on your destination, you may need to get familiar with practices that will help you to avoid getting parasitic infections. This might mean only drinking bottled water or using a special filtering system. It is also key to not attempt to travel when you are sick yourself. You could be risking the health of those you meet by exposing them to an illness their immune systems haven't encountered before.

Currency – In a majority of countries, you will need to change your country's currency into the currency of the country you are visiting. There is an exchange rate, which is the amount of your destination's currency you can get for your own currency. Typically, the exchange rate can be found online. Prices vary throughout the world, so it is important to know the exchange rate before you leave, so you can budget for each day's spending. You should also find out where credit cards can be used or if there will be any ATMs available.

Laws – Keep in mind that the laws as you know it in your country doesn't apply once you leave its borders. For example, if you plan on driving, then you need to find out how the driving laws might differ. You may need to have an international driver's license as well. Read up on the country to find out if there are any unusual laws that you need to avoid breaking unintentionally. Quarantine laws are another big area, as there may be foods or products that cannot be carried from one country to the next.

Research – No matter where you are headed, it is important to spend time learning about the culture of the country you are visiting. What might be a compliment or polite greeting in your home country could end up being an insult or rude in the country you are visiting. Brushing up on the locale can help you to have an enjoyable time as you immerse yourself into the culture and heritage of your destination country.

Language – I want to touch on language for a moment. Most of us are not likely to learn and be fluent in the language of the country we are visiting. After all, each language has its own unique rules and dialects, making it hard to pick up a new language in a relatively short period of time. However, you can learn some basic greetings, including key phrases. Don't hesitate to bring a portable dictionary, but there are also plenty of apps out there that can provide you a way to navigate the language of the country, including asking basic questions.

Immersion – If you are trying to really learn a new culture, then you need to be prepared to try new foods, begin the process of learning the language and find out about traditions and behaviors that are considered important in that country. At the same time, remember that you are a foreigner, which can bring its own unique risks. Crime, politics and other aspects can mean you will need to be more cautious in some countries. Find out where you need to avoid during your visit, including potentially high crime areas that should be avoided after dark. Check with your country to be sure there are no alerts against travel to your specific destination. While it may be only a caution, it is important to gather as much information as possible, so you can truly enjoy your cultural experience.

International Calling – In this day and age, we all have cell phones that serve as mini-computers. Before traveling, find out the costs for using your phones in terms of minutes and data. It wouldn't be a fun trip if you came home to a huge cell phone bill because you had to check in on social media multiple times in a day.

Documentation – Once you leave your home country, you will only have the documentation that you have brought with you. So it is key to make sure that you have your insurance cards, government id, and your passport. Additionally, you need to be sure that you know where to go if you need help, such as an embassy. There may be additional documents you need based on your destination country's laws, so be sure that you have everything before boarding your plane or boat.

Finally, take the time to get familiar with the weather patterns during the time you will be visiting. This will allow you to pack clothing appropriate for the conditions. You need to be aware that most airlines have a weight limit on your luggage, so it is key to pack just what you need and not over-pack for the trip.

| Electronics Around the World |

The reality of global travel is that there is no standard voltage. That means every country seems to have its own voltage, as well as specific outlet shapes. Just when you think you have the right adapter, you will find that it works for your laptop or tablet, but doesn't work for your hair dryer. Here's what you need to know before you pack up for your next international trip.

Over the last several years, most wall chargers associated with consumer electronics have been made to handle a variety of voltage, up to 240 volts. This means that if you can get the plug to fit into the socket, you are likely going to be able to charge your electronics. Years ago, North American electronics were able to only handle up to 120 volts, but the rest of the world had an input range up to 240 volts. Damage occurred when a North American charger was put into the rest of the world's outlets. Manufacturers finally got wise and decided to make the chargers adapt to the various voltage ranges found around the world. They didn't want to keep having to deal with warranty issues and irate customers when their electronics blew up.

Today, chargers are made with a worldwide view in mind, no matter who made them or where they were made.

That change is great for your electronics, but when it comes to your hair dryer, it isn't that cut and dry. These gadgets are also cheaper, so manufacturers are less motivated to make sure that they can handle the change in voltage. Therefore, to avoid smelling burnt plastic and having to buy a new hair dryer while you are traveling, it is important to purchase a voltage converter and a plug adapter. They are not necessarily expensive or heavy, but it will be two more pieces of equipment to account for.

Depending on where you are traveling, it might be worth it to considering using the hair dryers available in the hotel. However, if that won't be available, consider using a dual voltage hair dryer. Just remember to switch the voltage before you start using it to avoid any potential hazards.

There are plenty of things to consider when traveling, but once you have done all the homework, packed carefully and gotten to know more about your destination, it is time to go and enjoy yourself, while expanding your world view.

| Fun in a Foreign Country |

Now that we have talked about all the cautions, let's talk about what makes foreign travel so exciting. When you hop on the plane for your first trip, you are off to experience something completely new. There are opportunities to try new foods, especially those delicacies that are only available at your destination. The views can be incredible, especially if you are going to a country near the sea or by a fabulous beach.

There are opportunities for historical excursions or trying new activities, such as a local dance lesson or climbing a mountain to take in a spectacular view. These are just a few of the amazing things possible when you travel outside of your home country. If you choose to take advantage of an all-inclusive package, then your resort will typically also offer shopping, spas and a taste of home.

There are plenty of spots geared toward the tourists, but don't be so quick to avoid them. They can give you a bit of the flavor of the country in a way that you can easily understand.

However, there is nothing like the chance to go see where the locals hang out and enjoy their culture and customs up close and personal. Just keep in mind that you want to take someone who speaks the language, if at all possible. Guides are key to truly exploring and learning about a city or culture. They can help you to avoid potential faux pas and, at the same time, explain the meaning behind movements, dances, songs or even gestures.

The music of the country you are visiting can also speak to your soul. There are also opportunities to observe religious ceremonies as well, thus deepening your understanding of the spiritual culture of the country as well. Countries do not develop in a vacuum and it is clear that we all impact each other, both as individuals and populations.

Traveling allows you to see that there is more to our world than just our little corner of it. We also have the opportunity to open our eyes to another viewpoint or way of thinking about the choices of governments and leaders. The impact on us personally can be life changing. Ask those who have made one trip and found their calling or even decided to move altogether to a new country and make a new life for themselves. The possibilities are endless, but only if we are open to exploring our world and all the variety in it!

I chose to end the book discussing travel, but it is clear that there are so many aspects to having a VIP life. When it boils down to it, you need to be willing to listen, to learn and to act. Listening to yourself and others can give you the knowledge and insight to make big changes in your life and the lives of others. There is no telling what you can accomplish when you are willing to open your mind and heart to the possibilities.

I would love the opportunity to work with you to develop your VIP life. Contact me through my website, **www.gotTHEpowers.com**, and together we can explore all the ways you can be the VIP of your own life!

www.gotTHEpowers.com

BONUS
THE 10 THINGS YOU LOVE ABOUT ME

| **Bonus -** The 10 Things You Love About Me |

No matter who we are, love is a key ingredient to living our best and most authentic lives. How can we benefit from that key? Simply put, we need to love ourselves, including all the good, bad and ugly parts. We need to accept ourselves as we are and make changes that will help us to grow. Here are 10 reasons that you need to tell yourself every day to remind yourself why the ones in your life love you. My list isn't exhaustive, so please feel free to add to it. You love me because:

1. **I am unique –** In the world, there will never be another individual who has exactly the same experiences, knowledge and feelings as we do. Even twins don't experience the same situation the same way. Remembering your unique place in this world can remind you how much you bring to the world.

2. **My smile –** The smile is a way to convey so much emotion, including happiness and joy. When we take the time to smile at others, and ourselves we can encourage our own positive outlook on life. It is a powerful action, despite the fact that it involves just a few of our muscles.

3. **Loyal friendships –** No matter where we live and work, we are constantly interacting with individuals and creating connections. Some of those connections become friends that last throughout our lives. These loyal friends support us through the good and the bad times. Are you a loyal friend? If so, then that is something that people love about you.

4. **Your laughter –** When we laugh, we are actually healing others and ourselves. Laughter has been shown to relieve stress and help us to maintain our overall health. It truly is the best medicine. Take the time to laugh with your friends and others. You will be amazed at how much you all benefit. If you are known for your laughter, then you are sparking something amazing in others.

5. **Your spirituality –** We all have a need to tap into something greater than ourselves. When you explore your spirituality, it impacts how you view the world and can help you to find your place in it. During times of stress or tragedy, it can also be a source of comfort and growth.

6. **Positive attitude –** When others display a negative attitude, it is harder to spend time with them. Those who exhibit a positive attitude naturally draw us to them. Their joy is infectious. How is your outlook? What is the outlook of those you spend the most time with? You will be amazed at how their outlook can impact your own!

7. **Generosity –** Let's be honest. When someone calls us a skin flint or cheapskate, they rarely mean that in a good way. Those who display generosity typically win us over much sooner. Do we have a giving spirit toward others, even when it doesn't necessarily benefit us to do so? You will be amazed at how good it makes you feel, but when others are generous with us, it warms our hearts.

8. **Gratitude –** When we show our gratitude to others, it just makes them appreciate us even more. There are so many areas that we can grow and change, but without gratitude, it can be hard to appreciate all the ways in which we are blessed.

9. **Don't quit –** Not everyone has a don't quit attitude, but when we do, then we aren't scared by challenges or failure. We can brush ourselves off and come back to try again. The results are often amazing when we don't stop trying and the success is often all the sweeter for the effort we put in.

10. **Problem solving –** As we gain experience in the world, our ability to problem solve grows as well. It is easy to see that knowledge is power, but at the same time, our confidence grows when we are able to tackle and overcome a challenge. Problem solving is a skill that we can love about ourselves.

While this doesn't not cover everything that make us special and defines us as individuals, this list can help us to appreciate what we bring to the world. Don't hide who you are under a bushel, but let your unique light shine. You have the ability to make the world a better place, so get started!

| The 10 Ways to Get Rich Quickly and The Easy Way |

Growing your net worth is not easy. It takes action and effort on your part. I can help you to create a VIP net worth. Here are just a few ways to increase your net worth and change your financial future.

1. **Take risks** – When you are setting financial goals, it is going to require you to consider alternative methods that will involve risk. Don't be afraid to take a risk, because you could be missing out on a big return.

2. **Do your homework** – Before you invest, do your homework and know what you are investing in. Understand the potential loss and returns, so you are prepared for anything that comes your way.

3. **Own a business** – It may take work and investment, but owning a business can give you a significantly greater net worth. Those who want to increase their financial outlook are doing so with business ownership.

4. **Rental income** – Buying rental properties can create a passive income stream that can build your net worth. Depending on where you live, it can also be a great way to reduce your tax burden.

5. **Consider an internet business** – The internet provides multiple business opportunities, but only if you are willing to do the work. Still, it can mean that your website is working for you 24/7, versus a business with open and close hours. Thus, you are creating a natural source of passive income.

6. **Build equity in your home** – Making a slightly larger mortgage payment each month can help you to pay your house down faster and also build equity. That equity can be a key part of your net worth.

7. **Partner with an established business** – Buying a franchise system can give you the benefits of a system that is proven to work and corporate backing, while still giving you the ability to own a business of your own.

8. **Work hard** – While everyone wants to see their wealth increase with minimal effort, the reality is that you will have to invest some hard work in terms of time and effort. However, the results can be worth it.

www.gotTHEpowers.com

9. **Set goals** – If you don't have a financial plan, it can be hard to reach your goals. Set goals and then create a path to achieve them. When you do so, you can create milestones that will guide you to reach your financial dreams.

10. **Change your outlook** – When you are willing to look outside of the box, you will be surprised at how many opportunities can present themselves to you. Be positive and open to those opportunities. They can help you to achieve the goals that you have set for yourself.

Growing your wealth and finances is about more than having good spending and saving habits. It also means being willing to step outside of your comfort zone. When you do, there are many opportunities that will present themselves to create your VIP net worth!

| The Top 10 Ways to Enjoy Your Life |

Enjoying our lives is up to us. There is no one in the world that can make us happy or is responsible for our choices. Here are 10 ways to make sure that you are doing the right things to make your life amazing.

1. **Travel –** When you step out of your familiar world, you give yourself a chance to gain a new perspective and grow. Experiences make us better and deeper individuals. Travel helps us to meet those individuals who can give us a greater understanding of cultures and social expectations around the world.

2. **Read –** Taking a trip in a book exercises your imagination and allows you to travel the world from the comfort of your favorite couch or chair. Reading allows you to explore our world, regardless of your budget.

3. **Set goals –** When you have goals, it is amazing how much further you can go in your life. Without goals, it can often feel as if you are standing still and you may find that you regret it later in life.

4. **Spirituality –** Regardless of whether you believe in god or just a higher power, we all have a spiritual side. Exploring your beliefs can help you to deepen your understanding of yourself, as well as help you to let go of beliefs that you no longer agree with. You will also come to a deeper understanding of the world and your place in it.

5. **Nurture yourself –** Take the time to care for yourself. When you do, it allows your batteries to recharge and to reduce your stress. Find activities that relax you and allow you to de-stress. Your body and mind will thank you!

6. **Change your outlook –** When you have a positive outlook, your mind and body handle stress differently. Additionally, you will have a different perception of the world, allowing you to see change as a positive, instead of something to be feared.

7. **Choose your company wisely –** We are the company we keep. If we hang around negative individuals who invite drama into their lives, it will become part of yours as well. By making smart choices in your friends and those who you spend the most time with, you can surround yourself with individuals who will support you and your positive outlook. Positive relationships can be energizing, but negative ones can be draining.

8. **Try something new –** If you don't expand your comfort zone, you won't know what you could accomplish. At the same time, you can't grow if you aren't willing to try new activities and experiences. New hobbies can help you to make new connections with individuals who share similar interests as well.

9. **Meditation –** This is not about emptying your mind as much as it is about reducing the level of noise inside your head. Meditation offers you different strategies to quiet your mind and relax throughout the day. Depending on what you prefer, there are plenty of meditation methods available. Taking the time to practice it on a daily basis can help you to make it part of your routine.

10. **Journal daily –** When we are dealing with stressful situations, it can be hard to process our thoughts and feelings. Journaling helps us to do that by getting our thoughts onto paper. Once they are on paper, it makes them easier for us to deal with. This can also ease our desire to dwell on them and roll them over and over in our mind. Once they are on paper, it can be easier to let them go.

No matter where we are in our lives, these steps can help you to find the enjoyable life that you crave. Experience life and don't be afraid to step or jump out of your comfort zone!

| The Top 10 Ways to Enjoy Your Wife |

Marrying your wife is a choice you made because she enriched your life and hopefully, you enriched hers. But years of marriage, kids and the stress of life can take a toll on your relationship. Here are some ways to enjoy your wife and ignite your relationship.

1. **Plan a date** – When you were dating, you made time for each other. Marriage shouldn't change that. Plan a fun activity together or even just dinner with each other out of your traditional environment. It can give you a chance to talk about more than schedules and bills.

2. **Give her flowers** – A woman loves to feel appreciated. Flowers are an inexpensive way to show that appreciation and she sees it as tangible evidence that you see what she contributes to your family.

3. **Send her to the spa** – A wife spends a majority of her time focused on those around her. Force her to spend some time caring for herself by gifting her that time. She will recharge and everyone around her will benefit.

4. **Explore her interests** – It might not be your thing to sit at a play or go to a craft store, but spending the time with your wife doing an activity that she enjoys can draw you together. The bonus is that by stepping outside of your comfort zone, you may find an activity that you both enjoy!

5. **Travel together** – Learning about a new culture or just getting to see a new place can build memories that you both will look back on fondly. Shared experiences draw individuals together, but it can also help you learn more about each other.

6. **Laugh together** – When couples laugh together, they reduce stress. Often, the top things individuals look for in their partners is a sense of humor. Give her a chance to express hers, but try to make her laugh from your own antics. Laughter has many benefits for both of you!

7. **Volunteer together** – If you both get a chance to volunteer together, you can experience the joy that comes with helping others. It can also help you both to count your blessings and find the stress relief that comes from focusing on others over your own difficulties.

8. **Set goals** – When you set goals together, you build a sense of team with your mate. It is amazing how your relationship improves as you reach goals together and celebrate your achievements as a team.

9. **Dance** – Even if you have no rhythm, spend time dancing together. Slow dances or even being silly can give you a chance to be physically close and can create moments for laughter. All of these things can have a positive impact on your relationship.

10. **Explore your spirituality** – As a couple, you may each have different perspectives about spirituality. Take the time to explore your points of view. When you listen to your wife, you may find that she influences you to a new way of thinking and that can be a blessing in and of itself.

These are just a few of ways that you can grow your relationship with your wife. At the same time, this is not an exhaustive list. The most important thing to remember is that no relationship is stagnate. Activities and making time for each other can help your relationship to continue to grow and mature!

| The Top 10 Ways to Enjoy Your Children |

Children are a blessing. For those who want and are able to have a family, every child brings unique joys and challenges. Still, most parents would trade their children for the world, no matter the challenges that raising children can present. The day-to-day world often tries to interfere with that parent-child relationship, because parents are often so stressed out from handling the needs of the family that they may miss those important bonding moments. Here are ten ways to enjoy your children throughout your life!

1. **Communication** – It seems like a no-brainer, but communication is often one of the first things to breakdown in a parent-child relationship, especially as the child begins to assert their independence. While it might be hard, make time to sit and talk with each other. Those chances give you the ability to better understand your child and make it more likely they will feel comfortable coming to you with their own challenges.

2. **Find a hobby** – Finding a hobby that both of you enjoy doing together. This will allow you to build memories with your children. These are also times when memorable conversations can occur, simply because you are both out of your traditional environment.

3. **Plan a trip** – Go somewhere as a family. This break from work, school and everyday life is key to reconnecting with each other.

4. **Find a new activity** – Is there something that you have always wanted to try? Take your kid along and do it together. The chance to spend time with your children will never come again, so take advantage of every opportunity.

5. **View it from their perspective** – No matter what the activity, take the chance to view it from their perspective. Learn about animals as if it was the first time. Be in awe of the sunset with them. When you see their joy, it can only magnify your own.

6. **Tell them you love them** – Kids may not admit it, but they need to know that you care. When they have that sense of security, they find it easier to stand on their own two feet against bullying and negative influences. You are their biggest cheerleader, so let them know it!

7. **Be affectionate –** Take a moment every day to hug and be affectionate with your children. They love it and you will find that it lightens your mood as well.

8. **Be there for the big moments –** Kids remember when their parents showed up and when they didn't. Show up for the big moments, graduations, games and various shows. It might seem like a lot, but your kids will be glad you made the effort!

9. **Stand your ground –** It can be hard to stand up to your kids when they are pushing your boundaries. But standing your ground will benefit you both in the long run.

10. **Let them try –** It can be hard to let them try a new activity, especially if they aren't not instantly successful. Those failures can help them to build their character and know how to stand back up in the face of a challenge. You will be cheering them on when you see them succeed, but will be proud because they worked hard and earned their success.

When it comes to parenting, no child comes with a manual. Be willing to apologize when you need to and reassure them that you will always love them. Doing so can make memories that you will cherish long after your children have moved out on their own.

| The Top 10 Ways to Enjoy Travelling |

Travel is a great way to expand your horizons and experience a variety of cultures, places and meet new people. For many individuals, traveling is truly an adventure that invigorates their spirit and inspires them in their everyday lives. Traveling builds memories that last a lifetime. Still, there are those who have had horrible experiences traveling and would avoid it if at all possible. Here are the top ten ways to turn travel from a chore into a joy.

1. **Plan ahead** – So many of the headaches of travel come from not being prepared. If you are traveling out of the country, this preparation is even more critical. Make sure that you have done your homework on the documents, vaccinations and currency that you will need. Get to the airport early and give yourself enough time to get through security without having to rush. When you take the time to plan ahead for various stages of your trip, you reduce your stress and increase your chances to just enjoy the experience.

2. **Study up** – Whatever your destination, take the time to learn a little about the history or culture before you go. It can make your trip more enjoyable. Plus, it can deepen your experience and expand your perspective.

3. **Don't overbook** – It can be tempting to plan an activity for every minute of the day, but doing so will just leave you drained and not having a good time. Plan one or two activities at most, but give yourself plenty of time to just relax and enjoy your destination.

4. **Pack light** – When you have a lot of luggage to check and keep track of, it can add to your stress. Instead, keep your packing light and minimize the amount of luggage that you have. Additionally, packing light means taking what you need, but not a lot of extras. Remember, most places you go will have clothes or other necessities, so there is no need to pack for every possible scenario. Most of the time, it is likely that you end up over-packing in the end.

5. **Take a map** – While the world has become more dependent on GPS, the reality is that not every road in the world has been mapped. Having a guidebook or a hard copy map of your destination can be helpful when you are looking for your next stop.

6. **Travel alone** – There are some trips where it is better to take them by yourself. If you are visiting a spiritual retreat or just want the chance to meditate and take in nature uninterrupted, then traveling along can afford you the time to enjoy activities that appeal to you without having to accommodate a larger group.

7. **Travel with a group** – While there are times and trips that will be better when taken alone, some trips can be best enjoyed with a group of friends or family. These trips build the memories that are the talk of family gatherings for years to come. If you have children, these trips are the experiences that will shape their worldview. Be willing to expand their horizons and your own!

8. **Try something new** – Traveling somewhere new can be an enriching experience, but only if we are willing to step outside of our comfort zone. Try a new food, take a ride on a zip line or climb a hill and get a different perspective. It will make the trip memorable, while contributing to your personal growth!

9. **International calling** – If you are leaving your home country, make sure that you have made it possible for your cell to make and receive calls during your trip. Also, be sure that you know how much it costs, so you can limit your phone and data accordingly. While all those pictures and videos are amazing, it might be better to post them after you get back onto your home soil.

10. **Inform someone of your itinerary** – In this day and age, it is key that another individual, preferably someone not traveling with you, be aware of your destination and your plans. If there is an emergency at home, they need to be able to contact you quickly, which might not be so easy to do if you are traveling internationally. Having contact information for your hotel and main activities can make it easier if something were to come up.

Traveling is an amazing experience. It can broaden your perspective of the world and even help you gain a better idea of how to live within it. With these key tips, traveling can be an experience that you look back on with a smile and as an inspiration for your own personal growth.

| The Top 10 Ways to Have Better Sex |

While we spend a relatively small amount of our lives actually engaged in sex, it plays a large part in the overall happiness of our relationships. When the sex is good, our satisfaction with our partner increases as well. Yet, when it isn't working the bedroom, our relationship seems out of sorts in other areas. How can we improve the quality of those bedroom moments, so that happiness will bleed into other areas of our relationship? Here's my top 10 ways to have better sex!

1. **Be spontaneous!** Sex gets boring if we don't spice it up. One way to do so is to not plan to have sex, but let it happen spontaneously. The truth is that our willingness to open up to sex at different times and in different places will spark our partner and make sex more interesting.

2. **Listen** – When you listen to your partner, you can find out what inspires them in the bedroom. If they can see that you are listening, then it will deepen your intimacy and your sex life will benefit.

3. **Be romantic** – A great sex life starts outside of the bedroom. Being romantic with your partner, including telling them how much you love and appreciate them, can be a great way to grow your relationship.

4. **Thoughtful gifts** – It warms our hearts when others take the time to give us a special gift. When we see that they were thinking of us and the gift has a personal touch, it is even more endearing. Being that thoughtful with our partners will make them feel appreciated and benefit your bedroom as well.

5. **Put your partner first** – What does your partner need? If you do your best to fulfill their needs, they will reciprocate and you both will win!

6. **Don't hide** – If you are feeling hurt or frustrated, it doesn't help to keep it to yourself. Share with your partner what you are feeling and experiencing. When you do, the intimacy between the two of you will grow.

7. **Bring the kitchen into the bedroom** – Everything that is good for you above the waist is good for you below it. The best foods are ones that are high in protein and low in fat, as well as high in antioxidants. Another bonus is that food can become part of your foreplay, making the whole experience more exciting.

8. **Change up the location –** Sex doesn't have to be limited to the bedroom. Try a different room or even take the action to the shower. It can create excitement and intimacy at the same time. Also, consider options that bring in the potential of being caught, as it can bring added excitement.

9. **Build the mood –** It is not appealing if you have to race to get time alone. Instead, doing a little planning that allows you to set the mood with candles, favorite foods and even special outfits. Setting the mood can build the excitement, making the whole experience better for both of you.

10. **Don't always have intercourse –** While that might seem counterproductive, it can actually make the experience more fun. Do things to give each other pleasure without intercourse. Set a time frame beforehand, so that you both know when it will be back on the table. It will help you both explore each other and grow even closer.

These are just a few tips to improve your sex life. The truth is that you need to build intimacy with your partner to achieve the best sex for both of you. Talk with your partner and open the lines of communication. You will be amazed at how much you can benefit as a result!

| Author Bio |

Susan Powers was born and educated in the United Kingdom. She developed a love for buying and selling at a very early age. After leaving school, she gained several years' experience in the retail profession before becoming a highly successful entrepreneur and business woman. She has developed an in-depth understanding of all the skills and personal requirements necessary for success in the modern world.

Susan focuses on helping her clients master the skills and become better versions of themselves. She is passionate about her work and committed to helping people discover their true worth in life. Her approach is both unique and creative in achieving the best results for people in a way that is fun and inspiring.

Susan Powers is a successful entrepreneur business owner, consultant and author. She currently lives in the United Kingdom and provides consulting services to her clients, who achieve their VIP lives.

Be healthy, wealthy and wise with Susan Powers Creative Consultancy at ***www.gotTHEpowers.com.***

| Testimonials |

"When I met Susan I was immediately impressed by her intellect, enthusiasm and charisma. I have enormous respect for her attitude to life and her ability to communicate her ideas effectively. She is an excellent speaker and motivator who pushes people past their fears and inhibitions to achieve their goals."
Dr Alan Cushway, Consultant Metallurgist, Birmingham, UK

"After retiring from a long career in local government I worked with Susan Powers to establish my own Media Services Consultancy. Susan's energy, enthusiasm and commitment have been invaluable in enabling me to make the most of my skills and experience and successfully return to the workplace."
Chris Maddox, Media Consultant, Birmingham, UK

"The Susan Powers Creative Consultancy personal shopping service is first class. My wardrobe has been completely transformed without breaking the bank."
Samanther Brookes, Lady of Leisure, London, UK

"I was made redundant and spent a long period of time unemployed. I contacted Susan Powers Creative Consultancy and working one-on-one with Susan I developed a 'return to work' strategy. My C.V. was revised and updated and my interview technique analysed and refined. I have now secured a position in the financial services market."
Adrian Price, Financial Advisor, Sheffield, UK

"For anyone seeking a fresh look and expert advice on beauty products and treatments look no further than Susan Powers Creative Consultancy beauty breakfast club. Thanks to Susan I feel and look years younger."
Chloe Townsend, Housewife, Cheltenham, UK

www.gotTHEpowers.com

Made in the USA
Charleston, SC
29 November 2016